BITCOIN WHALES

*Guys Who Fooled The World, Secrets
and Lies in The Crypto World*

Alan T. Norman

Table of Contents

PREFACE

If you, my friend, are reading these lines, then I must be dead... Just kidding). It's a positive way I decided to start my story about one of the greatest Batmen of our time in. Without the greatest discoveries of this miracle of man, I would not write this stuff now, and you wouldn't read it accordingly (for some reason, the spirit of Richard Pryor still does not leave me:-) Well, we can discuss serious things with a humorous undertone as all jokes have truth to them, and our "joke" has a great deal of though unproven but still truth. So put your funny rose-colored spectacles on and let's go off on a journey under the slogan "Intelligence."

My previous books (which you have read, I hope) were devoted to Blockchain, Bitcoin, cryptocurrency trading, hacking and other screeds. And one fine evening, while drinking Dominican rum by the fireplace, a brilliant idea came to my mind: to stop torturing you with complicated stuff and start writing about simple things. Namely, about the most ordinary person who did not quite an ordinary thing - he invented the protocol of the first cryptocurrency. Every dog in my and your neighborhood knows pretty well the name of this man. We will talk about Satoshi Nakamoto.

And here, folks, the most interesting story begins: despite the fact, even your granny knows the name of this guy, no one has ever seen him. But wait: have you seen him in person? No? Me neither!

Did this Satoshi simply appear out of nowhere, do good for you and me (after all, Bitcoin is good, right?) and quietly return to himself to the other world. It is difficult to understand why he prefers to take a backseat and not to rest on his laurels and bask in the glory. He could at least gain more followers on Instagram or YouTube and advertise some kind of toothpaste, couldn't he?

In any case, the personality of Satoshi Nakamoto still remains undisclosed, and I am sure that this story looks a bit dull to you. Since I've loved to poke around shit since my very childhood (I mean "shed light on the questions which are difficult to find answers to"), I decided to make some inquiries in this issue as well. If you are the same kind of restless bro, as I am, then let's go and root around this shit (crossed out) conspiracy theories together. And our journey looks very exciting, believe me.

In order not to wear you down with the stories only about one man, I've decided also to tell you about my investigation into some jiggery-pokery in the cryptocurrency market (yes, bro, you read it correctly - jiggery-pokery). They all lie – starting from stock exchanges and ending with a specific cryptocurrency. Be patient, you will find out everything.

A creative person inside me doesn't want to turn this scribbling into a work deprived of talent, so I framed my investigation into the "Play" genre. We will puzzle out the number of acts in it later, and now I can present you the cast of characters:

- Mr. Satoshi Nakamoto himself
- Geeks, who created Blockchain with faith in bright future

- Eggheads, who opened the first centralized exchanges for decentralized currency (sounds like a tongue-twister, yeah?)
- HFT traders[1], who discovered a new world cryptocurrency
- Banks, which learned to solve their problems (far from the Blockchain), using cryptocurrency
- OTC[2] dealers and their ability to save money of bigshots

So, take your popcorn, make yourself comfortable and let's go!

P.S. All pictures from the book in high quality and size you can find here **http://bit.ly/btcwhales.**

---

[1] In financial markets, **high-frequency trading (HFT)** is a type of algorithmic trading characterized by high speeds, high turnover rates, and high order-to-trade ratios that leverages high-frequency financial data and electronic trading tools.

[2] **Over-the-counter (OTC)** or **off-exchange** trading is done directly between two parties, without the supervision of an exchange. It is contrasted with exchange trading, which occurs via exchanges. A stock exchange has the benefit of facilitating liquidity, providing transparency, and maintaining the current market price. In an OTC trade, the price is not necessarily published for the public.

CHAPTER 1. SATOSHI NAKAMOTO, LET ME SEE YOU!

How well it all began...

The project called "Bitcoin" was created in 2009 by a certain Satoshi Nakamoto (or by a group of people under the pseudonym Satoshi Nakamoto). This man simply posted the informational materials on the network in which he described in detail his decentralized currency. Later, he also opened the first cryptocurrency wallet and launched the network itself.

Although Satoshi Nakamoto is called the creator of Bitcoin, it is worth noting that 90% of the development in this field had been done by other people before him. Nevertheless, Satoshi came first in:

1. Bitcoin's name
2. The idea of Bitcoin usage

At the dawn of its existence, it was very easy to mine Bitcoin and it cost almost nothing. Anyone could install the appropriate software and "create" hundreds or even thousands of Bitcoin for themselves. In a cushy time, no one thought that Bitcoin would reach almost $20,000 in distant 2017. And since those people couldn't dip into the future, they were squandering their Bitcoin right and left. It will just suffice to mention a story of an American guy, who bought two delicious pizzas for BTC 10,000. Oh, yummy)) The guy enjoyed pizza worth several million dollars at current rates! But that's another story.

Bitcoin started its way with very loud statements. Let's remember them (or commemorate, LOL):

- Decentralization: the inability of anyone to influence the currency in any way
- Irreversibility of transactions: no one is able to cancel or block transactions
- Anonymity: it is almost impossible to establish the identity of a person who committed this or that transaction
- Availability of cryptocurrency for beginners: for example, cryptocurrency emission occurs through computer calculations, so anyone having a more or less normal computer can create a little cryptocurrency for themselves.

So what do we have in sum today and who really stands behind all the sounding promises to mankind?

The interest of the society in Bitcoin's creator increased in sync with the growth in the popularity of cryptocurrency, but the final answer to the question "Who this Satoshi Nakamoto is?" and whether he exists at all has not yet been found. All that we know about a Bitcoin developer is his nickname on the site. The user was active through a system of proxy servers, allowing to preserve the anonymity of the network connection. The profile also indicated the information that the user lived in Japan and at that time he turned 37 years old.

To clarify the image of this ghost man, I will use two his personal little articles of memoirs (he wanted to be famous, you see). Therefore, I formally express my gratitude to Mr. Nakamoto for the information provided, which greatly helped my investigation. For me, it was not just a set of letters, but real food for thought. So really, brother, ta much!

So, all the material you will read below is based on only two sources:

- Bitcoin Whitepaper (an article of Satoshi Nakamoto published in 2009, *https://bitcoin.org/bitcoin.pdf*)
- A book by Mr Nakamoto (*you can find it on amazon*)

I will exclude from these sources boring information like the SHA-256 algorithm, this book is not about such abstruse things, so folks, do not worry, pour a glass of wine and continue reading.

So, the first clue in our investigation is provided by Mr. Nakamoto himself, who, despite all his desire to remain anonymous, gave himself away as he got confused in time zones when he had been posting on social media and forums. It turned out that the guy wrote not from Japan, but from the east coast of the USA. If you doubt it, then know that it's not my guess. Satoshi himself told about this "blunder" in his book.

What else did Mr. Nakamoto tell us about himself? He is scant of words about himself in the book, but still: he said he worked as an IT laboratory assistant at some institute, and his mother was engaged in writing at that time, but apparently she had not been good in it as Satoshi noted that she had been unpopular (much less than others, yeah? :) Satoshi was in his twenties or thirties when he created Bitcoin.

Nakamoto also noted in his book that English is not his native language. However, someone edited his texts! His mother, perhaps?

Alma mater

The identity of mysterious Satoshi Nakamoto has always prompted journalists to somehow wild assumptions as many people have been considered creators of Bitcoin. There was allegedly even some sort of evidence. Australian Craig Wright, American of Japanese origin Dorian Satosi Nakamoto, Professor Nick Szabo, Irish student Michael Clear... It is not the whole list of possible creators of Bitcoin. But we are not on the bit of assumptions of others but carry out our own personal investigation. So, put your diving suit on and let's go deeper.

In view of the previously discovered facts about Satoshi Nakamoto's place of residence, I first had to remember which cities belong to the east coast of the United States, which are: Boston, Portland, Providence, Hartford, New York, Newark, Buffalo, Albany, Philadelphia, Baltimore, Washington, Richmond, Norfolk, Raleigh, Charlotte, Columbia, Charleston, Atlanta, Savannah, Jacksonville, Orlando, Tampa and Miami. Since our Satoshi misspoke that he was an IT laboratory assistant at some institute, we should find all the universities with IT education in the neighborhood. I used website study.com: Purdue University, Ashford University, Georgetown University, Baker College Online, Strayer University, Regent University, Capella University, Lincoln

Tech, City University of Seattle, The Art Institutes, Lewis University, Virginia College, Penn Foster Career School, Saint Joseph's University, Penn Foster High School, Utica College, Brightwood College, The University of Scranton, Colorado Christian University, Fortis College, University of Delaware, CDI College, Altierus, Stanford University, Harvard University, University of Pennsylvania, Duke University, University of Notre Dame, Vanderbilt University, American National University.

Do you think I'm mad enough to snoop around all these universities? Yes, I know that I'm crazy a little bit, but not so much! It's easier for me to find another far more "mad" dude, who did this job before me. I found such a man on bitcointalk.org (*https://bitcointalk.org/index.php?topic=58590.0*). And what did this guy do? He found 114 male students, who searched in the network at their universities the information about cryptography. I want to note that at that time (in 2012) the book of Nakamoto had not been released yet.

Here is a list of the names of potential IT students:

1. Adhikari, Avishek   Indian Statistical Institute, Kolkata 2004
2. Applebaum, Benny   Technion-Israel Institute of Technology   2007
3. Arrighi, Pablo   University of Cambridge   2004
4. Avoine, Gildas   École Polytechnique Fédérale de Lausanne 2005
5. Aydos, Murat   Oregon State University   2001

6. Baier, Harald — Technische Universität Darmstadt
2002

7. Bak, Daniella — City University of New York
2000

8. Barak, Boaz — Weizmann Institute of Science
2004

9. Batina, Lejla — Katholieke Universiteit Leuven
2005

10. Benits, Jr., Waldyr — Royal Holloway, University of London
2008

11. Bentahar, Kamel — University of Bristol
2008

12. Bisson, Gaetan — Technische Universiteit Eindhoven
2011

13. Bisson, Gaetan — Institut National Polytechnique de
Lorraine   2011

14. Bone, Eric — Brandeis University — 2004

15. Boneh, Dan — Princeton University — 1996

16. Brassard, Gilles — Cornell University — 1979

17. Bregman, Ido — Hebrew University — 2009

18. Broadbent, Anne — Université de Montréal
2008

19. Cachin, Christian — Eidgenössische Technische Hochschule
Zürich 1997

20. Chandran, Nishanth — University of California, Los Angeles
2011

21. Chee, Yeow Meng — University of Waterloo — 1996

22. Chor, Ben-Zion — Massachusetts Institute of Technology — 1985

23. Ciet, Mathieu   Université Catholique de Louvain   2003
24. Cohen, Aaron   University of Minnesota-Minneapolis   2007
25. Condie, Leisa   University of New South Wales   1992
26. Cusak, Charles   University of Nebraska-Lincoln   2000
27. Damgård, Ivan   Aarhus University   1988
28. Dechene, Isabelle   McGill University 2005
29. Desmedt, Yvo   Katholieke Universiteit Leuven   1984
30. Dodis, Yevgeniy   Massachusetts Institute of Technology   2000
31. Döring, Martin   Technische Universität Darmstadt   2008
32. Doumen, Jeroen   Technische Universiteit Eindhoven   2003
33. Eagle, Philip   Royal Holloway, University of London   2008
34. Fernández Rúa, Ignacio   Universidad de Oviedo 2004
35. Freeman, David   University of California, Berkeley   2008
36. Freking, William   University of Minnesota-Minneapolis   2000
37. Gastaud Gallagher, Nicolas   Georgia Institute of Technology 2007
38. Giuliani, Kenneth   University of Waterloo   2005
39. Green, Matthew   The Johns Hopkins University   2008
40. Greenfield, Jonathan   Syracuse University 1993
41. Grundy, Dan   University of Kent, Canterbury   2008
42. Gysin, Marc   University of Wollongong   1998
43. Halsey, James   North Carolina State University   1970
44. Hardjono, Thomas   University of New South Wales   1991
45. Heindl, Raymond   Clemson University   2009
46. Henhapl, Birgit   Technische Universität Darmstadt   2003
47. Herzog, Jonathan   Massachusetts Institute of Technology 2004
48. Hitt, Laura   University of Texas at Austin   2007

49. Hsiao, Chun-Yuan   Boston University Graduate School   2010

50. Juma, Ali   University of Toronto   2011

51. Kaliski, Jr., Burton   Massachusetts Institute of Technology 1988

52. Kalka, Arkadius   Ruhr-Universität Bochum   2007

53. Kanukurthi, Bhavana   Boston University Graduate School 2011

54. Kaps, Jens-Peter   Worcester Polytechnic Institute   2006

55. Karabina, Koray   University of Waterloo   2010

56. Khadra, Anmar   University of Waterloo   2004

57. Kiayias, Aggelos   City University of New York   2002

58. Klima, Richard   North Carolina State University   1997

59. Klimov, Alexander   Weizmann Institute of Science   2005

60. Ködmön, József   University of Debrecen   2005

61. Koskinen, Jukka   Lappeenranta University of Technology 1994

62. Kumar, Sandeep   Ruhr-Universität Bochum   2006

63. Laskari, Elena   University of Patras   2010

64. Liskov, Moses   Massachusetts Institute of Technology   2004

65. Livne, Noam   Weizmann Institute of Science   2010

66. Lu, Steve   University of California, Los Angeles   2009

67. Mashatan, Atefeh   University of Waterloo   2009

68. Maurer, Ueli   Eidgenössische Technische Hochschule Zürich 1990

69. Minder, Lorenz   École Polytechnique Fédérale de Lausanne 2007

70. Mironov, Ilya   Stanford University   2003

71. Möller, Bodo   Technische Universität Darmstadt   2003

72. Monico, Christopher   University of Notre Dame   2002
73. Montanari, Andrea   Università degli Studi di Perugia   2010
74. Moran, Tal   Weizmann Institute of Science   2008
75. Myers, Steven   University of Toronto   2005
76. Nance, Jr., John   North Carolina State University   1972
77. Neat, Charlie   University of California, Los Angeles   1975
78. Overbeck, Raphael   Technische Universität Darmstadt   2007
79. Papakonstantinou, Periklis   University of Toronto 2010
80. Park, Je-Hong   Korea Advanced Institute of Science and Technology   2004
81. Park, Seung Kook   University of Illinois at Urbana-Champaign 2007
82. Peralta, Rene   University of California, Berkeley   1985
83. Peters, Christiane   Technische Universiteit Eindhoven   2011
84. Petkova, Maria   Humboldt-Universität zu Berlin   2009
85. Qu, Chengxin   University of Wollongong   2000
86. Ràfols, Carla   Universitat Politècnica de Catalunya   2011
87. Rhouma, Rhouma   École Nationale d'Ingénieurs de Tunis 2008
88. Ritzenhofen, Maike   Ruhr-Universität Bochum   2010
89. Rodriguez-Henriquez, Francisco   Oregon State University 2000
90. Savas, Erkay   Oregon State University   2000
91. Schaffner, Christian   Aarhus University 2007
92. Scheidler, Renate   University of Manitoba   1993
93. Schillewaert, Jeroen   Universiteit Gent 2009
94. Schwabe, Peter   Technische Universiteit Eindhoven   2011
95. Shaheen, Rasha   Cairo University   2010

96. Shang, Ning   Purdue University   2009
97. Shen, Shuo   Purdue University   2007
98. Shershin, Carmen   University of Miami   1982
99. Shokrollahi,   Jamshid   Rheinische   Friedrich-Wilhelms-Universität Bonn   2006
100. Sigmon, Neil   North Carolina State University   1995
101. Stebila, Douglas   University of Waterloo   2009
102. Sunar, Berk   Oregon State University   1998
103. Tawalbeh, Lo'ai   Oregon State University   2004
104. Teague, Vanessa   Stanford University   2005
105. Thomas, Tony   Indian Institute of Technology, Kanpur   2006
106. Toli, Ilia   Università di Pisa   2004
107. Wehner, Stephanie   Universiteit van Amsterdam   2008
108. Weis, Stephen   Massachusetts Institute of Technology   2006
109. Wolf, Christopher   Katholieke Universiteit Leuven   2005
110. Wolf, Stefan   Eidgenössische Technische Hochschule Zürich   1999
111. Wyseur, Brecht   Katholieke Universiteit Leuven   2009
112. Yao, Chui Zhi   University of California, Riverside   2008
113. Zuccherato, Robert   University of Waterloo   1997
114. Zumbrägel, Jens   Universität Zürich   2008

Link on the structured table

Now let's sort out why we should take into account all these guys from the list above:

- Nakamoto says in his book that he needed knowledge of mathematics and cryptography
- Nakamoto anonymously published his post on Bitcoin but he could not lurk when making cryptographic requests in his native alma mater
- Nakamoto confessed that he had created a prebitcoin before Bitcoin, so he persistently studied cryptography for this purpose in 2007-2008, which means he made web requests at the university
- Since he lived on the eastern coast of the United States and worked as an IT laboratory assistant at a university, it makes sense that he did his requests from the same place.

Out of the considerable number of guys (potential Satoshis), we should leave only those, who were not just looking for information on cryptography on the Internet but were studying at the universities in the US east coast. We have only six of them left.

1. Cusak, Charles   University of Nebraska-Lincoln   2000
2. Mironov, Ilya   Stanford University   2003
3. Monico, Christopher   University of Notre Dame   2002
4. Shang, Ning   Purdue University   2009
5. Shen Shuo from Purdue University 2007
6. Teague, Vanessa   Stanford University   2005

Do you know how to further narrow the circle of these potential "Satoshis"? Select only those, who studied at the university in 2007–2009 and there are only two such persons:

- Shen Shuo from Purdue University (2007);
- Shang Ning from Purdue University (2009).

Shen & Shang

Since we have not a great number of the candidates for the title of Satoshi Nakamoto, only two, let us delve into their biographies.

Shen Shuo wrote a thesis[3] on the elliptic-curve cryptography back in 2007. You may ask what it has to do with Bitcoin. I will answer that the link is direct since Bitcoin uses elliptic-curve cryptography (*https://en.bitcoin.it/wiki/Secp256k1*) when creating a public key (addresses of BTC wallets).

The academic advisors for this thesis were:

- Professor Samuel Wagstaf (Purdue University)
- Doctor Michael Jacobson (University of Wyoming)

The second dude, *Shang Ning*, wrote his thesis[4] in 2009. What was his topic, any ideas? Of course, it was the effect of snails on the formation of ozone holes! No, spooky you, his topic was the elliptic-curve cryptography, like the previous bro had.

The academic advisors:

- Professor Samuel Wagstaf (Purdue University)
- Professor Andreas Stein (University of Wyoming)

I'm not patient enough to analyze the theses of these two dudes (someone will claim I'm not brainy enough), therefore, as a genuine egghead, I only looked at the beginning and the end of the theses.

---

[3] http://www.cerias.purdue.edu/apps/reports_and_papers/view/3210
[4] https://www.cerias.purdue.edu/assets/pdf/bibtex_archive/2009-07.pdf

Thus, at the beginning of his work, Shen Shuo expressed his gratitude to his family - his wife and child. But Satoshi was a little over 20 at that time, so what is the likelihood that the guy already had a family at that age? As for me, it is quite small, and Shen Shuo was older then.

In turn, Shang Ning thanks only a certain Mary Gitzen, who helped him with English when he had just moved to the USA. And we remember that Satoshi Nakamoto had troubles with language (English, bro).

In the thesis by Shang Ning, I noticed another interesting thing: he writes about the "time-bound hierarchical key" and, as far as I have enough brains, this is a time-related cryptographic key. At the same time, the description of the encryption algorithm is given by the example of vendors and subscribers, and this already suggests a similarity with Bitcoin as a means of payment.

Now let's go back to the Bitcoin Whitepaper. We can find such a block there:

3. Timestamp Server

The solution we propose begins with a timestamp server. A timestamp server works by taking a hash of a block of items to be timestamped and widely publishing the hash, such as in a newspaper or Usenet post [2-5]. The timestamp proves that the data must have existed at the time, obviously, in order to get into the hash. Each timestamp includes the previous timestamp in its hash, forming a chain, with each additional timestamp reinforcing the ones before it.

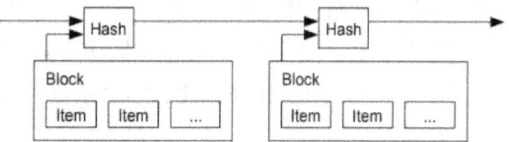

Don't you think that Time-bound hierarchical key and Timestamp server have the same concept? Nakamoto argues that it is the Timestamp server that solves the issue of protection against "double spending" of cryptocurrency assets.

In addition, I found another parallel between the thesis of Shang Ning and Bitcoin technology. The thesis described a new method of cryptography called "polynomial parameterization", which was also mentioned in one work on Bitcoin (*The Bitcoin Backbone Protocol: Analysis and Applications, https://eprint.iacr.org/2014/765.pdf*).

Now, a few words about the "shady past" of both dudes. Shen Shuo was born in Fuxin in northeastern China. In 2000, he received a bachelor's degree in mathematics at the University of Science and Technology of China. At the Purdue University, he received a Master of science degree in electrical and computer engineering. In 2007, he defended a thesis on cryptography, which we have already analyzed.

Shang Ning was born in Anyang city in Henan Province. In 2002, he received a bachelor's degree in mathematics at the Wuhan University. In 2007, he received a Master of science degree in electrical and computer engineering at the Purdue University. In 2009, he defended his thesis on cryptography, which was the subject of our discussion.

The moral of the fable is...

I will not give anyone the run around for too long and will finally quench your thirst to hear the real name of Satoshi Nakamoto. So drum roll, please ... my guess is that he is Shang Ning.

You will say: Yes, of course, Shang Ning! Why not Zun Pun Sun or Dai Hui? Keep cool, bro, now I will explain all the points:

- In 2007-2009, Shang Ning, like Satoshi Nakamoto, stayed on the eastern coast of the United States;
- Shang Ning is not an English native speaker. In his thesis, he thanked for help a certain Mary Gitzen. For Satoshi Nakamoto, English was also not native, and he also thanks to the woman, his mother, for teaching him. And who knows his mother's name?
- Shang Ning studied maths, computer technology, and cryptography, and Satoshi Nakamoto argued that those skills are fundamental for creating Bitcoin
- Shang Ning writes in his thesis about the practical application of cryptographic algorithms with vendors and subscribers (does this remind you of a transaction?). The same is described in the Bitcoin Whitepaper
- Shang Ning was under the age of 30 at the time of writing the thesis, as Satoshi Nakamoto was.

In conclusion, I also decided to rummage around Linkedin Shang Ning (*https://www.linkedin.com/in/syncom/*). Here is a screenshot below:

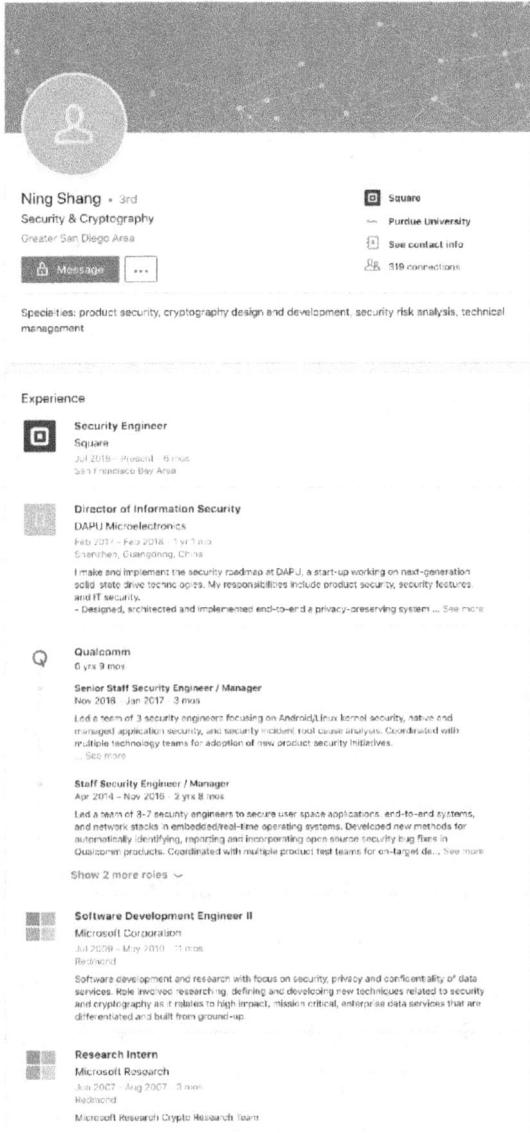

His profile confirms that the dude is working persistently in IT sphere:

● He had been a member of the Microsoft research crypto research team (https://www.microsoft.com/en-us/research/group/cryptography-research/) and worked at Microsoft research even before he defended his thesis

People

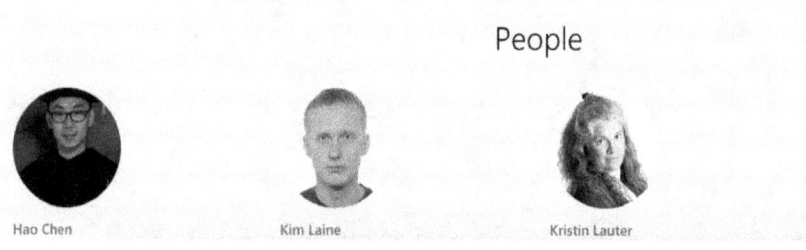

Hao Chen   Kim Laine   Kristin Lauter

- During the period of study at the Purdue University (2007-2009), he did not work anywhere, and we remember that Satoshi Nakamoto created Bitcoin at that time

- Shang Ning defended his thesis on January 1, 2009, and the first Bitcoin block was created on January 9, 2009. Already in July of that year, he returned to Microsoft for the position of Software development engineer II

- In 2010-2012, he moved to the position of Senior security engineer at Qualcomm. He later moved to the position of Chief security engineer

- February 2017 - February 2018, Shang Ning served as a director of information security at DAPU Microelectronics
- From July 2018 up today, our Satoshi Nakamoto is just an ordinary security engineer at Square. A Private engineer!

Are you serious? People usually tend to a rising trend in their careers, and our Satoshi turns out to prefer the downward trend? Here is another interesting fact: the office, which Satoshi now works in, is engaged in hardware and software to express credit card payments. Perhaps, we should closely monitor this company, since Bitcoin is also means of payment!

This is where my first fable ends. Who knows whether I found Satoshi Nakamoto or it is just another attack of acute schizophrenia. One reader will be sincerely happy about this news and run to preach it all over the world, while another one will decide to send me some pills against insanity. By the way, if you also have a desire to send me something, then I accept Bitcoin, not pills. Really, bro. Do not be embarrassed! Write me an email and I will send you my wallet's address (Let me explain for some serious readers: "I am joking":-).

By the way, an editor of the Forbes USA once admitted that the journalists of their media outlet spent about 10,000 hours on searches for the identity of Satoshi Nakamoto but failed to gain any results.

In a word, whoever this dude, who created Bitcoin, is, I deserve the journalistic Oscar (if any, LOL) or a bullet in the forehead for my investigation:)

CHAPTER 2. FROM THE FIRST BLOCK TO THE FIRST EXCHANGE

So, in the previous section of the book, we went to the end of the earth to get super-agent Satoshi Nakamoto. If his personality conceals so much interesting things, then imagine what is happening on the vast cryptocurrency market, what incredible secrets and manipulations it hides from our eyes. But we are not simpletons, right, bro? And, therefore, we will dig out the truth! So, we will start our research from the era of the dinosaurs - the first mined blocks – and will move towards the appearance of the first cryptocurrency exchanges. Without making this way, you will never be able to understand the market and, the more so, to trade (and it is a very profitable thing, believe me). If you feel suddenly that you have already matured enough and are ready to memorize not just the words "cryptocurrency" and "Bitcoin" but also such abstruse phrases as "Elliott waves" or "support and resistance levels", you have found the right place.

I'm not sure you will easily perceive all the following information, so take another glass of sparkling wine (or some more) and continue to read.

As I have already mentioned, I decided to start my investigation from the period of mammoths. In the world of cryptocurrency, this period was when the first 1,500 blocks were mined. I decided to examine those blocks on my own. They certainly belonged to Satoshi Nakamoto as they were mined in the first month of Bitcoin existence. I also began to study all the wallets from which the first Bitcoins were transferred somewhere.

Are you sure you are mentally resilient enough to see my work? Well, then have a look at the list of wallets)

№ of Block	Reward BTC	Recipient, who was SPENDING
9	50	12cbQLTFMXRnSzktFkuoG3eHoMeFtpTu3S
78	50	1AiBYt8XbsdyPAELFpcSwRpu45eb2bArMf
309	50	1627A2DbCtVVykWVJmdQz2ERwkw4uiEL22
317	50	1E5npMTmh9PnBHxCacuqzAZRGEybkxPMAq
320	50	12V3D1ytYGZgYTgmuNh8JLAiKMF9chUoDd
329	50	153h6eE6xRhXuN3pE53gWVfXacAtfyBF8g
357	50	18KrJNtPVu6LWRNPQReqF29iFm7vDhirMk
360	50	18SH9vwx24L5cTabfkgtGMjF8A56pD9AUJ
361	50	12wej8tANWruTQFEhWFJtTkjNLt76pE268
372	50	1PQjPXAtSZfUiiQeD4nafQ7HKx7J1kYQ4J
394	50	1JV9ZQX6cCd4YrUtHHQm9iDL6cMxP3oQ3J
407	50	1PEsXxy7kVSPL3Sqw9q4HPkbM368tGTYcx
413	50	15ATbhqgqxkGen8ZLsb2BEbQzw3ymdzbQ9
417	50	1ELmSkQWnqgbBZNzxAZHts3MEYCngqRBeD
419	50	19CkFSEiHB5UVah3fvZD17qk48m82TfAp8

431	50	1ADpf5rHERc2PmVAZZFoH7WbougKvkPDVD
433	50	1ajo3LNjjNWK7GMJwa71tcR3Mk6roeaS9
439	50	1PxUJBokfT8Cn1pizWYeJpbpm9To4HwRHr
442	50	1ACWHyRM8rtbt96KauPJprnF2qDQSdPJ54
450	50	1LfjLrBDYyPbvGMiD9jURxyAupdYujsBdK
461	50	15Eto1LeCTkZGkPwr3H2BS8Nu1yadfeEH8
463	50	13Vpu2cTr58iTAKaF9MfYxrgzYTHK64qtG
465	50	1xgLCvWYJGuCxqPunbBiUxmSKLDwxZeu5
473	50	17c6L9JUGVenn6CfqXuB93L3Tk8Tbzefui
490	50	15ALyVo8ZuoTikHMYRq6p8nGr17gxQApXf
493	50	1L9kYwPr6SWvp8zsxvJARHt4UUVk51WQcf
501	50	132aSc15WmoPwtMbqRVzouZKNnjWL1YTVb
506	50	17oofDoUGPaTi7xEP3StP1sU1YxEMDfQa6
509	50	1Miuw7ifaTYY5qrzKYFcTDiojSFxRfAqwP
512	50	16cHAjKh6Gr5HFDqz6JKgLmtpMzbKpZYfa
521	50	1CrnUia9wfeNFbdwKJNj89YqA6qetvYTTE
528	50	12oRSUW6UVYNCUk8yyrFvbpbJw7uia31sA
541	50	1JCNTEzhK5J8dPhhsnarS3UeQe7rxgmZig
562	50	17k3Gr1KM16X5cQ5VCp7sBmw12Gh9bpL6m
563	50	1CnKmNvgA4aK8LhKiKekNnnHcqeFpwGUbU
567	50	18bN2GBzfRwnV6dmr7MiuDoxn39uqvjwPs
575	50	1LVcDpgziv9d6hXKF9ncYveDdQWb1j88m8
591	50	1PmxdAq9UdYqB8TL45asUeV4PxTLiTuNiw
596	50	1CpZmPEGBbH7gUsM1xS31CvaKDE92EiiKg
598	50	1HKqNPMm1yjNb2YaAuTG8VcQ3hUCfgCPob
607	50	1D1FUseiHmbRPDCRvExrBX3C3BtFxGimMz

614	50	15qgGqvzsyCYnjyCQLNrXzjtgxQvGVLPj4
624	50	1LtEkbFPkXouhn9uUyYbaGwUEF4AUazuR5
651	50	14nELEgJL95NU3BKi5D734ysFuVUCEjLWg
658	50	1KZXdVqEtWUpq1BRb1S69kfgszLbn8t1vt
666	50	1C1QnL6oZqiRmKgaTm8XZbHccwupvJsAwG
685	50	1ADTuxdhYePCW9PEvkCKnib6jmbg6mKXdz
687	50	1M7kUuZDyHT5opZr789ybEES6Nyqxxyk6T
688	50	1GEhNKRWcePnKDhAieuAAcW6FkwDNZqKX7
699	50	1Nsyx1KBDfTCczg2LmXu2HagyfewQkSPH9
702	50	1MqispkLBvCEwxq2dwzXdgMR97v8VJjYUH
707	50	1HZKjpAYdaiXvCV3b6mXExrhPd3djzDWM
720	50	1P9JXnCX3wzHXgHtpPgkAg2DX25e3HTkEk
726	50	1Q6kHNUDra29FqKGXf8rWuj6LZizjAHVvq
728	50	1EDym1P2XMxJVuWaEt7BaPL5B9AijhhD4K
730	50	17C8uaaknVNSfGM6eeaZQzrrEuhveQPirv
739	50	1NyD2gM5qcGCRKmuJK7gUUqcQMrUFQRZQz
748	50	16HRfyssnLAtnpWG8pnGJdGgNpXtKW78Yw
752	50	1DdhxvYwVrnUP4xcWaquUnmZ177HVeUT2L
757	50	1DayUvccL8WV7zjkn26aC3M4hwGwJFyFw4
767	50	19QiFoYFBf8bo6STnvdCD21ASskDGkpaSQ
772	50	1BGnWwafsPsHo11opJGVbJdLADxakwZoAD
773	50	1MxQgXvgUuSj7ScRwuJ3p4t9rstnd3NqFv
777	50	1Gg5WVQsrfk8L9uMpmtsFqW7NoS2ZpoKPs
782	50	1HnKDtdn1Q7qLh8rC722c5af6RhSsnHbSE
786	50	1PyKe5Dokd9T6WMq1Wjc4mZ99v88dCKJWe
803	50	1DCcZbNtttndh6tvoK8xRTB5BUMdfL51aL

809	50	1HG3byV85t3wiZ4uazZJvntRQT2Rmw4rbm
813	50	1Bs54ogGcFTejhoyNwDgJR9x7yRHHnv1JF
814	50	1Fz1PZ4m2PykPasegmG3oWNXTu837Buu8T
819	50	17LDnEt8ggVjH43QdjhZ4FhkXC9zXgk48b
821	50	19oF5fxNiUDMr7FyZzyZhz9TxDdKGGkqUW
824	50	15fLMPJUAyiuc28gscdmRnVu1zUC1TXHtz
828	50	17jkFTQuYaGssazzqZ6CTHgRVQYRgLmf34
842	50	18QQUbHJhyzFDVKhEHPhHFZF3qdBmp74eB
850	50	15dnC28mA2tnbSbyjtqVRVtcmXwroDSrJQ
869	50	1CbDYwNDp5aA5FVmCf2Z95kjkMCgoBr2X8
877	50	1CPoDZcupzrLJCPvPovsyQJCgSjgwzHocD
885	50	1QNzY4rFXUrigUtbuvPu7wsKvHsDQKv86
905	50	1GZczj6uyZ1gyipBrNpN66cVvXnSbnESsH
913	50	18XcqBQ7BbE7TLvQfbGHKhqBgo4MvjGGVG
923	50	1MDDHENF1xDvN2C1a2HzvC3nuthsjXyLjL
927	50	1GHH9T1zinmfy8VqYcSuZP7qtCkGSPR44V
935	50	1JjyaJhj7gM1BDPjkKvNPp6zGQodneSRzW
940	50	1CsZEWqUk95GggXg1mvxP6qWv95bCvVaZs
945	50	1DGgqqQHfwGX28FzenC2DgqX2fzgU99urQ
949	50	12oAMNsu5qmzpcafSKJMYxnPCyaYxui4sp
955	50	1MJFHWKEZhTJkvw7Jygf9PnaSZRDdD8HLV
956	50	1L6yp2BegnXYnHCxm2CutMjrzHzDRmFEcT
958	50	16miRBBoGPbButAoZfxSMG4VgwoHrKUiCk
959	50	1LH3y6VPnF1KcPhxLSJ3eJ3NHvXWSaysAr
964	50	1FZooLsa7YyoSY8NUw1SDam7ZN6GghbJ76
966	50	1AoWi2xSyQoWuxrYrdr1PPVi5PxA8caNGC

979	50	17CtNkUdjYwa99vAHb9YbgXJ36wTRHQh3r
984	50	1CLK9m1s3D9Lc2oQprZ3jNdz9ikcdbH6vb
986	50	12VKdj1La4fnqX7qTQPfPwm9McBxtmtSsG
992	50	1PD7u8S27HS3PcY6ZKAM897RQLK5rx87wq
994	50	1MT2FEY48nq9qRcEQs43KKCbiZw1HNJg58
996	50	1A18WA52hdnHgGhgmd7yR6dgtnEhQrLnFJ
998	50	1AZBpyYUSWApQkKqsEDZ9mriWCZMArrgzR
999	50	1Ktq4ujHAwk8Utk1AGzCCq2aFBRbdkMeh7
1003	50	1A9VNjdMGHdMRhaHNj8zwRNLoutbDysvoU
1010	50	1PWjDwnVTSnSFzde8NpU7QRcVKJ4kAqtpE
1014	50	187TqctoDdtHaQDStEiRJGSPK93Yr45psE
1018	50	1NChfewU45oy7Dgn51HwkBFSixaTnyakfj
1025	50	15JuUHnBm5AtG4AYbSMVxHXrvdvMVubZrr
1027	50	152XPBGegp6jKSxYfEmhpzcnDQdrogc8dk
1031	50	1Ewy2mCVfDwGRBEDbFzHTMsDiCxTGLx72A
1042	50	1HQkgckTBytqaGmwyQgqTU5aptuZ7qFiyp
1063	50	1NdLg6FNKyFXyRfmFssW4DSgaWRzscYXUg
1068	50	13xWc32uuYEtXkMruFY8Ego4wP9ynBxmhB
1075	50	18RXG5o4g2dqZKbhorDcMAZHDdY5hn5V86
1088	50	13HyCUP3tdwUrQACdesNC6NCG99jXLFanc
1091	50	1NiUwRWvCEWBTHCNJAW9mGAk4AxwoXTj9J
1094	50	1AuUQiT2eBhJq4XPDBCvgDNszzAi8JoWro
1096	50	19NaaYCw1UBQd2gFfc77bKnVesA5d7fFzM
1102	50	12GXsmgDpTJC63NcK67Lvns8uLPWHe3Ari
1107	50	1B9zyacRvnw5CL6NBd3HN484eDNsQqFNyV
1113	50	1Cf8eqCMA26nNQysQ12cpWbyT15uSJ6TMu

1114	50	1J6AgPccDGJ9NdGD9RjnMM8zPvWmcMRpEX
1119	50	14zHfSpU4kbiqwqAHPm669SKe6HSbyKQkB
1123	50	15ac3UtBMowi6oDz82S1FXWq4RU48EZ3QN
1125	50	1qvpfJXzAzKJvkbBFRVEtNZw6yU31orDL
1135	50	1JNoSuNB7PVtMyeAy6nkNNcbubo4cDPPAS
1136	50	1675n6xp1aQ53w8kPJaghB749v5ekeyVGb
1139	50	1HaEeDfAWeo4hopjYMAx1At75uhY614C9X
1143	50	144KB1evSa1FjKEp9jBFKTznNREJLqvjvW
1144	50	1MUKXPFrGZNWeJApikyeK8VoFVTqmDLDHB
1150	50	1B7XbL6wMCPmCfwKtDgEdoSucWR4PYYBP4
1153	50	1BSgXqBzNHFfdqRHBPzLD23CFXpzhqpRrb
1178	50	17xz3mGXbf1D9Yz2FXwMTsUJs7oMcUUiTv
1192	50	1DGdXqZeQsMKwfEpbAuvPHt2d72jfk1VWG
1195	50	1GSAXEQEW7st7prSuz89x6DjKEcLUFSDCJ
1206	50	12BpQhir1LnPLoENAGAqwfW2X82kP1PCtw
1214	50	15w2oa5zs7EZNfamsvouyHdHP6ApCBUbWH
1217	50	16J5sZw9rZfcmPuHgp73exrbj37ierpuNQ
1218	50	1GNYTnnXzM2YNLXRGahfgVW5TkoHz6HuWp
1219	50	132FRJJLYxf4D94721mLqMR5CH3N6PzHUW
1227	50	1NRn1gzBWF2rKqUJBY37P1JgK1Zn4a1x9b
1233	50	1AHJbmcNpaxrgwDc12XFXnUSfpED5ksSiH
1240	50	1BtNBoKGgME9HCkjeHNJ6FrsZaAMTLCWED
1242	50	1Cndx9tcJHh2GGSnvG3nzsWmYMNxDMd61u
1245	50	1LNJ2Hx612Yf8uTxtojpTFPCniGHv2Aeok
1248	50	13kBLtgfK3uR7Ku87Co66xmgCZe67S674B
1254	50	1JDr5igrBmDC6zNtkqFrjpaPNb8wwLvYVz

1255	50	1JSnYFMbMbAB9hCT78WWAP32Hhc6EaVBSJ
1260	50	1B2HeTwi2y1aHXcLPZN5EePboJ3qTVbixT
1267	50	15j9aNE6D1ZnJF8Ags86vrkHbMGZBkroc9
1269	50	15aLEm1J4nZiLBEd5MmdRSj34MnF5GCaky
1270	50	1CGrQkozzohNKcUVGjMJH4UMcjjufmtnFq
1276	50	1DsGZxBbPXrLj5B8H39wJrVCTjYFKYRwXx
1284	50	15L3KzV9ZhiReTF8vvdRu7AwABTNjU7x1N
1285	50	1KKQHhasw82cjLidcrEFmcXavtXcja3qdH
1289	50	1FD2WQ9ov4b9czEFd9hJnMBcLfonJ8NcRq
1296	50	125JeyLib4bzAkqFbcidrNqwcty6S51yCu
1298	50	1NwocmtHDBp3uJNMXTyj7gTLXwvWZPMcrq
1299	50	1L4Ad5A1xw15cr6wkmEpHBYeMTSDEaVct4
1309	50	162T6BNdxfiMkTJssASmNW9Joat1Cy1PUH
1316	50	13evwJtdkEp2wcmv5xtqE7mF6pr5bFrbxw
1333	50	1M79wfuR7Bjgeu4DgfSP8G6E5Mpx2hqUhb
1342	50	1JFmQAS8du4V8JvZBpwXvMnzyhEXkC4b7N
1352	50	1MYDoS7PxsjYQveWRSHYLGf6KMe2gdsuM3
1376	50	14DFY3RsdrJ5U6CCgatYssM2gKAiyBm4mE
1378	50	1H5RfmcyUvJPSujfGLKRSp9G5nodt2nAxC
1383	50	1BGKfxaa8rMtKAsNXGMmAXmCeUFpe7pMxB
1388	50	1mCcDsmFi37DDr1Wv3t6bTpmc29uBJkJg
1389	50	1PpzwxQ3Uz9U2jZPuJQ8khoXJbyk51zb54
1390	50	13yawe8cxT5xaYLQ39rAnbUUxeFppNrBpM
1391	50	1NGqnHmn3W8XV7YujeL3LhnWwqQzzMmwr4
1392	50	1FqhgVCeyrwRrVSob8EUPPfqKfGhMgDr8e
1393	50	17raqeUa1C6DP1SYkN1QWUv5esnWpqfBZi

1394	50	1FgcFGzaAHVSkKxysugAg8CnsysjL4Pf17
1396	50	1GaVH6stCc4bwYkWe6VcRM24HHSszq85a4
1397	50	1BENJudbbZ8dfTwFtCLuJNWMTtBLE2bZa
1398	50	1LXgpvzVXBeiPaX8HLynZmib3968fiZHu7
1399	50	114rh9hzgStCRbXWuuahe87nQdkY1Ebncr
1408	50	1YBxWKBmTQvZKAWXwKuMHfRQd9Rzbw62v
1409	50	114Y2Hz7uDHmyK5iKhAzMbPZrHbYnNXqAX
1412	50	1By2YCAamR9incizhczhs6n1kfaEPy3cAM
1417	50	1KsUoXTpVc3cfW8rDdDXrunSSmSeMeGphf
1425	50	18VgUpjy6dTosH1LB2bvfsduJo3RuUCFwr
1440	50	19msR75aJX8Bn7TApWg58GSJp8r5YrMLWd
1471	50	1Jy5dQmet2xg1Pk5VYZE2hSWu8StK6aQWZ
1479	50	1K2rGvYh58r5kuTK6pSsizkN8uwhBFy7w
1486	50	1BKDLRuEy8uaKweNewFS41w7GUc41m4cDU
1487	50	1D3RX2nN4v5cE8GLPHqT7RWa8YVGvoAot7

Why are the first Bitcoins of Satoshi Nakamoto so interesting? The following fact is curious: everybody has long been convinced that these Bitcoins are fixed, that is, that they have not been sent anywhere. You understand, bro, I will not challenge this either)

So, the case is that Satoshi Nakamoto allegedly disappeared in 2010, but on June 19, 2011, one could easily trace the outgoing transaction from his wallet (1627A2DbCtVVykWVJmdQz2ERwkw4uiEL22[5]), which contained BTC 50 mined back in 2009:

---

[5]
https://www.blockchain.com/btc/address/1627A2DbCtVVykWVJmdQz2ERwkw4uiEL2 2

1. collection of cryptocurrency to the tune of BTC 2,000 from various Satoshi's wallets;

2. transfer of BTC 2,000 somewhere.

If you try to imagine what all those transactions looked like, they lined up in a labyrinth like this:

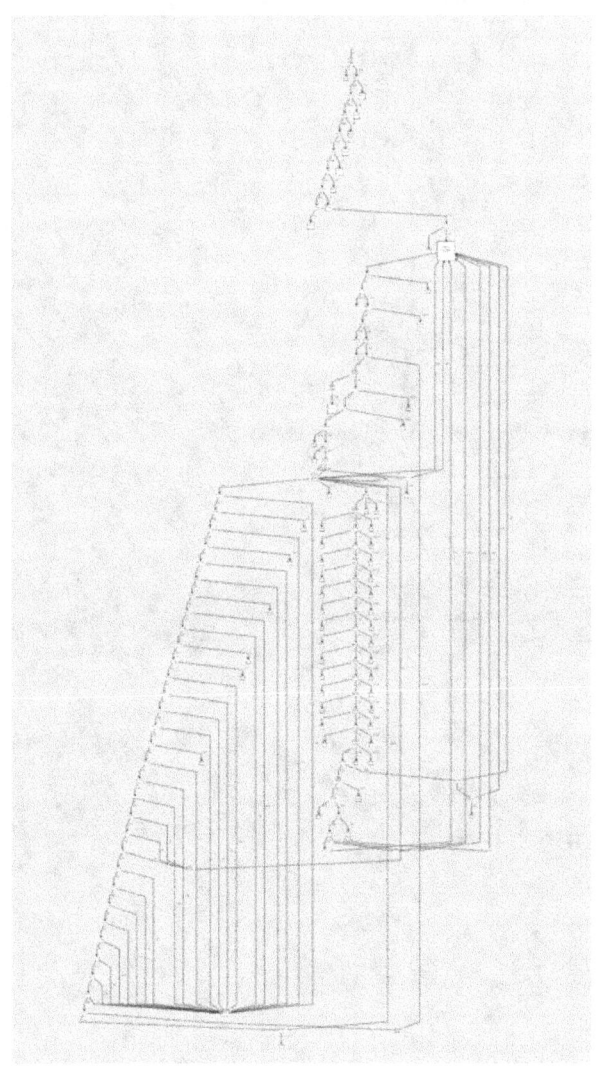

If you are even bigger crank than me, and you want to see the full horror of the labyrinth with your own eyes, go to this site (https://www.blockseer.com/), bro.

Special attention should be paid to such three interesting points:

1. the Theymos case (THEYMOS)

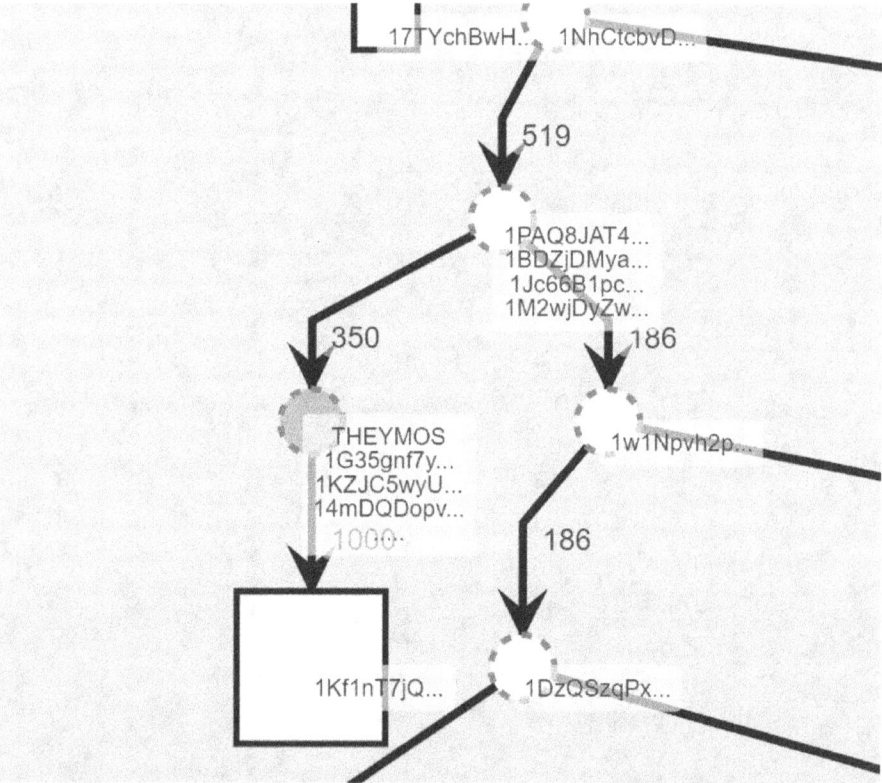

2. Nakamoto hub

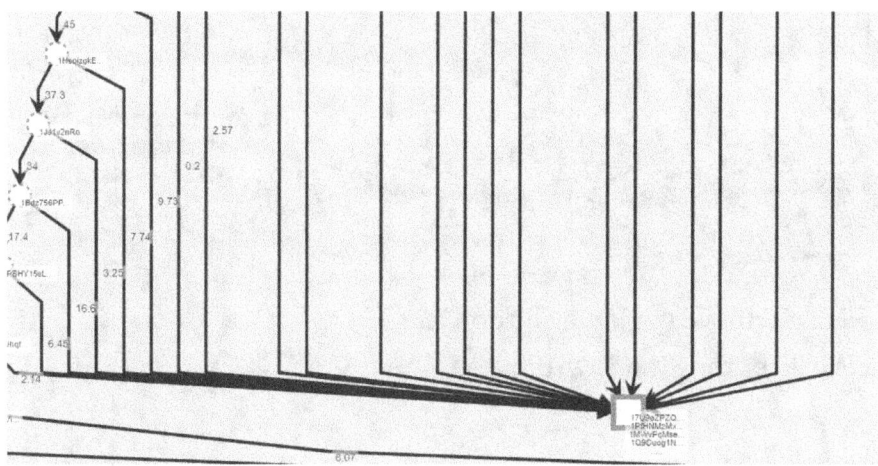

3. Big Guy wallet

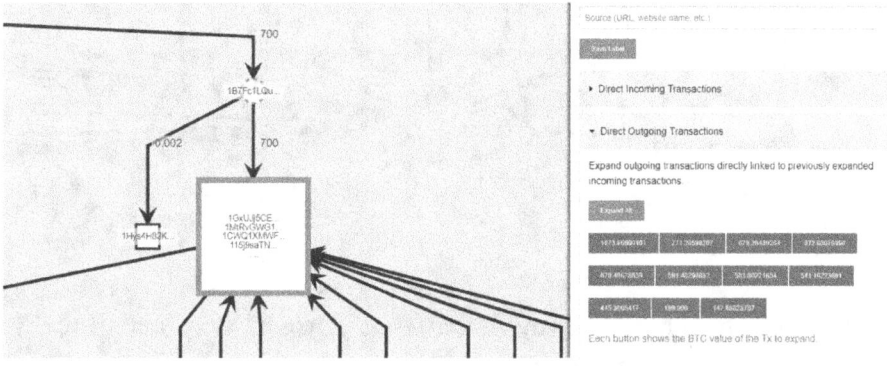

However, bear in mind that we have analyzed **just one address** from Satoshi Nakamoto's wallets! Just one, Carl!

To my mind, the most interesting one is Nakamoto hub, the outgoing transactions of which have the transaction of BTC 13.73804.

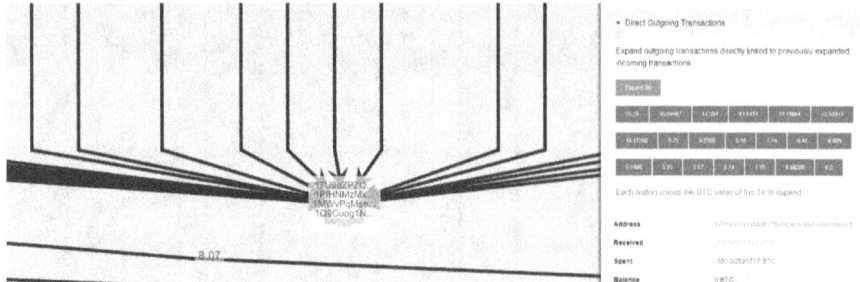

What will we get if we click on it?

We'll get the SILK ROAD!

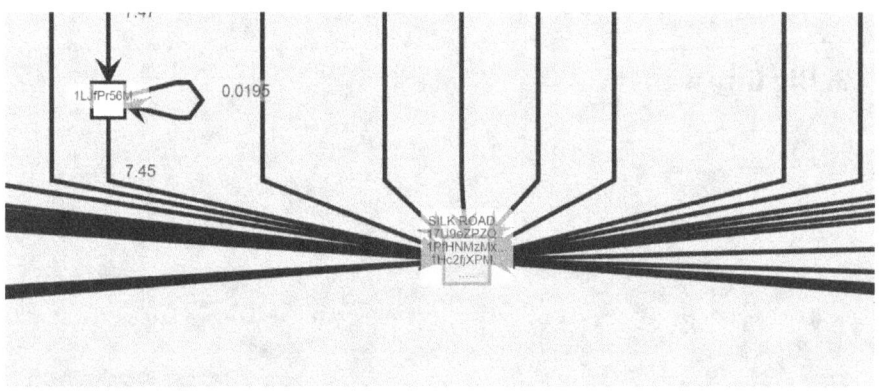

Of course, I have no evidence that Satoshi was washing his money through SILK ROAD back in 2013, but the fact remains.

Now let's go back to the wallet 127eQydc39bFw8jJMYrWJRwatJvntZWNfF, which I called the *Big Guy* as it contained thousands of bitcoins. The wallet looks like this:

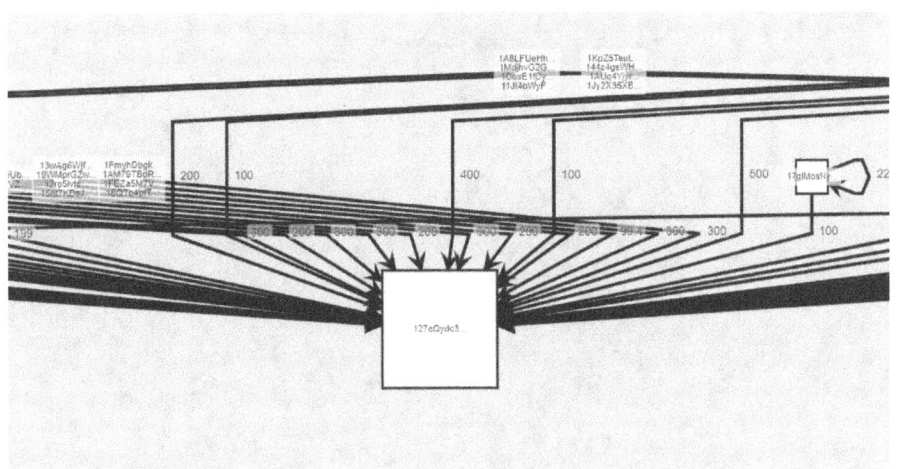

So, as much as BTC 32,360 went through the Big Guy wallet, and the last transaction was made on April 17, 2013. Having analyzed all the transactions of this wallet, I found a juicy carousel packing BTC 10,000 and transferring BTC 5-10 to different addresses each time. The carousel looks like this:

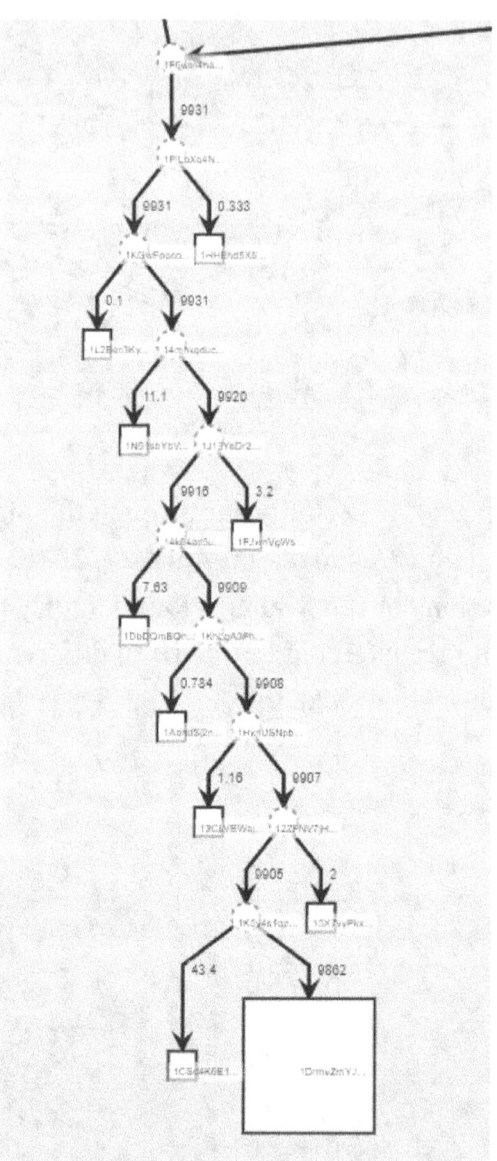

Then my brain got stuck (yes, it happens with cranks sometimes) and I decided that I was tired of analyzing through Blockseer, so I switched to blockchain.com and began to recheck all the transactions on transfers of BTC 10,000. Here are the wallets I found:

I was sitting stubbornly on my couch for one hour, then one hour more, and one more, and was looking at the moon. No, my friend, I was looking at how 10,000 diminished. Thanks to persistence (I bet the right word is *lunacy*), I managed to reach the end of the chain, where only BTC 20 remained from BTC 10,000. I got to the following wallet:

1PySs5yB9TU7toyTsrXKdT356gYmoSLMRw.

You may ask what is so special about this wallet. It is definitely special, bro. Just take my word for it. Wait, you'd better read)

This wallet is linked with two pools that are engaged in transferring BTC 0.00000001 as a warning about upcoming price change (it is my personal discovery, but the topic is so complex that you will read about it in my next books or find out about it in your next life). Here are the transfers I am talking about:

1. pool No.1 (7 October 2017)
2. pool No. 2 (3 April 2017)

Both pools worked from a wallet, which I call "Sochi" because of the first letters in its address (by the way, Sochi is a city in Russia). Looking at "Sochi", you can also see the "Enjoy." This wallet also makes a pool of transfers of BTC 0.00000001 (10 July 2017).

And now the drum roll: a chart is going to appear in my book for the first time. Yeah, baby!

I decided to put all three pools on the Bitcoin price chart. Look, what I've got:

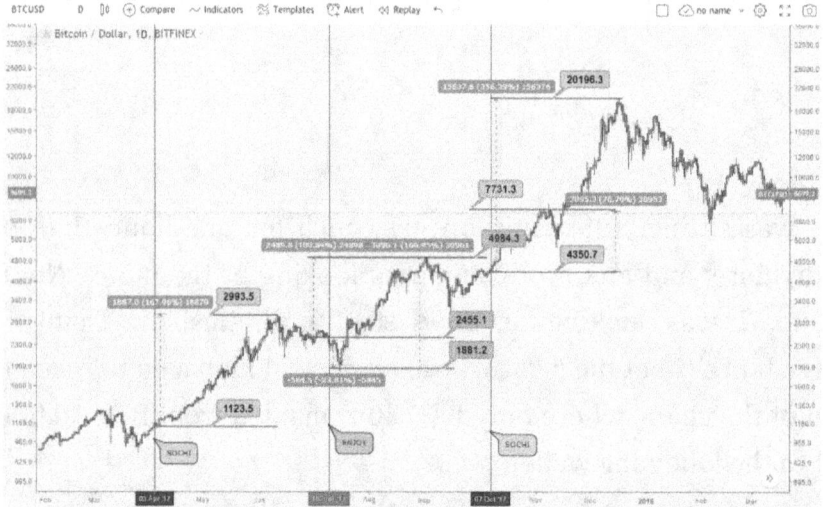

A very interesting coincidence: pool No. 2 preceded the Bitcoin price growth by about 166%, and the "Enjoy" pool preceded the price pullback by 24% and then growth by 166% began again.

Theymos got into a game

If you've read carefully, you should have noticed that we missed one moment: THEYMOS. Do not worry, you'll grasp everything)

First, Satoshi Nakamoto transferred BTC 350 to this wallet. Second, THEYMOS is one of the first Bitcointalk administrators, and the Bitcoin transfers were associated with the then Bitcoin Donations for Bitcointalk campaign.

If you analyze the profile of THEYMOS (*https://bitcointalk.org/index.php?action=profile;u=35*), you'll see that he is rather active on the forum, but it's not the point. Read here. The post was published back on 1 October 2015.

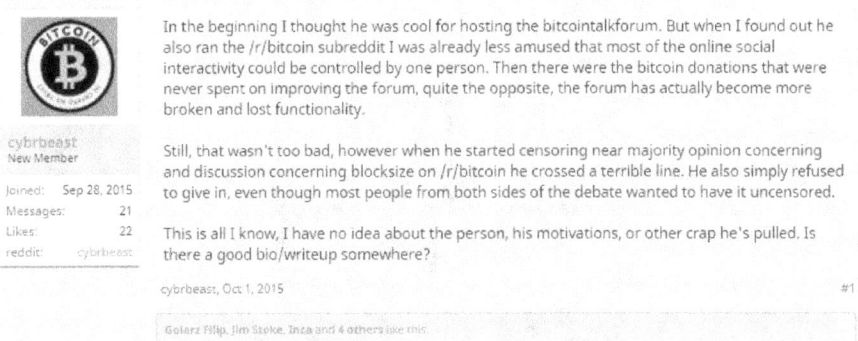

An administrator's response to these accusations was the following:

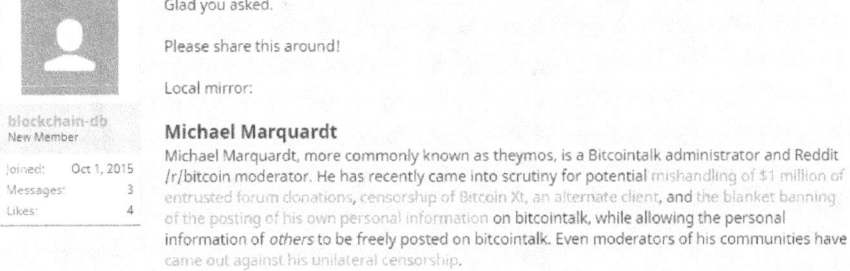

As it turned out, THEYMOS is Michael Marquardt! And now fetch this:

- wallet THEYMOS No. 1 -
  1NXYoJ5xU91Jp83XfVMHwwTUyZFK64BoAD;

- wallet THEYMOSNo. 2 -
  138eoqfNcEdeU9EG9CKfAxnYYz62uHRNrA.

Here comes the drum roll again:

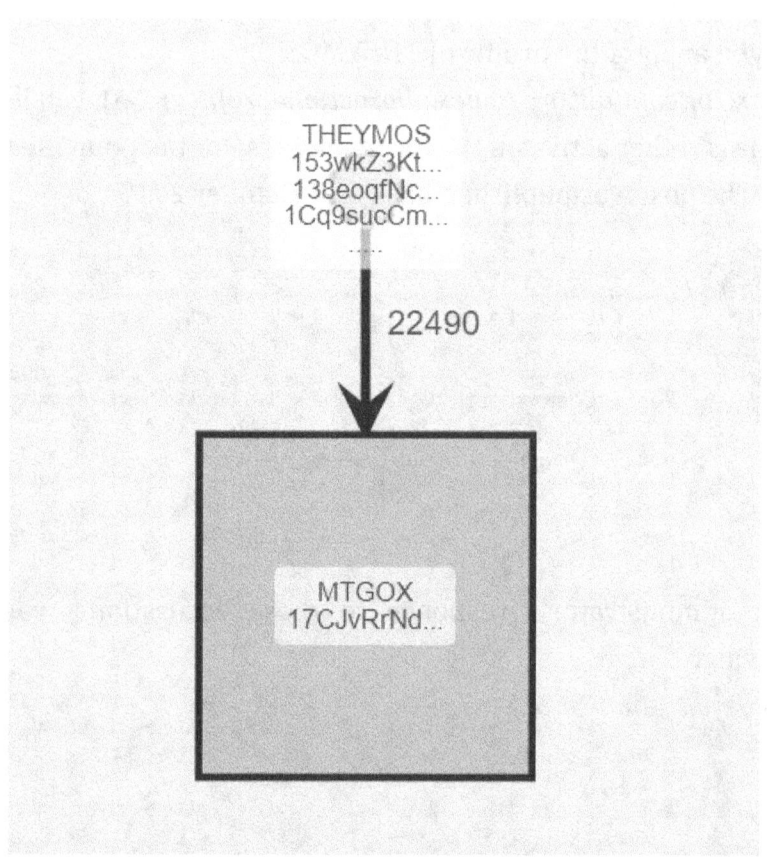

THEYMOS - MTGOX!

Hence THEYMOS became one of the first investors in well-known MtGOX (if you don't know what this thing is, then grab a reference:

https://en.wikipedia.org/wiki/Mt._Gox).

So, THEYMOS transferred BTC 22,490 to MtGOX. You can even check out this transaction here https://www.blockchain.com/btc/tx/d38f1409a188bc60b2 23ca329e05d53af8de249e95c169640b95be3319836be4. This transaction was carried out on 21 May 2010, and the official date of MtGOX's foundation is 1 July 2010.

Mt.Gox

Mt.Gox is an online Bitcoin exchange that facilitates the trade of Bitcoins for local currencies around the world.
Tokyo, Tokyo, Japan

Categories	Bitcoin, E-Commerce, Financial Exchanges
Headquarters Regions	Asia-Pacific (APAC)
Founded Date	Jul 1, 2010

Cut the crap, brah, I do not know how about you, but this makes me sick a little bit. Let's take a short pause before the next batch of interesting stuff. Meanwhile, you can read my conclusions in this section:

- Satoshi allegedly disappeared, but his money may still be moving
- Satoshi put his money into Silk Road mixing service
- Satoshi arranged a carousel, thanks to which we found "Enjoy" and "Sochi" wallets. A Russian city and Satoshi - are you serious, guys?

Satoshi transferred money to Theymos, and the latter turned out to be a deceitful man and invested all his capital in the MtGOX exchange even before its opening.

CHAPTER 3. EXCHANGE MTGOX

I feel you...
I feel your rapid warm breathing. Your purposeful glance from under the half-closed eyelids. Your soft fingertips, running through the hair and...

And a clear question in your head: "WHAT A CRAP AM I READING RIGHT NOW?"

Don't be mad, brah, it is not the next part of "50 Shades of Gray", don't worry. You have not gone astray. I just prepare you for the next shit (read "conspiracy"), which I have dug out in this miraculous decentralized cryptocurrency market!

In fact, I've just decided to make a sort of literary reboot for your brain. Have I succeeded in it? If I have, keep reading. If I haven't, I am lucky to be quite far from you now. Hold the book tightly, nerd, and read on!

So, as we have found out in the previous section, THEYMOS transferred BTC 22,490 to the wallet of MtGOX exchange on 21 May 2010. What kind of "office" is it? Let's figure it out.

MtGOX[6] was founded back in 2007 by a guy Jed McCaleb. At the very beginning, the exchange was engaged in selling Magic the Gathering (*https://en.wikipedia.org/wiki/Magic:_The_Gathering*) game cards, hence it was named Magic The Gathering Online eXchange. In 2011, the exchange was sold to the Japanese company TIBANNE Co., Ltd. Thus, Jed McCaleb ended up with only 12% of MtGOX shares, and a certain Mark Karpeles *(https://www.linkedin.com/in/karpeles/)* got the rest 88%. Even before the exchange was officially launched - as we remember on 1 July 2010 – money had started to hit its wallet:

---

[6] **Mt. Gox** was a bitcoin exchange based in Shibuya, Tokyo, Japan. Launched in July 2010, by 2013 and into 2014 it was handling over 70% of all bitcoin (BTC) transactions worldwide, as the largest bitcoin intermediary and the world's leading bitcoin exchange

Date	Amount BTC	Senders	Sent
19.05.2010	10	16RcAV7PN6QS3MaRtSEy3YbBfztA1DUxr	10
21.05.2010	22490	153wkZ3Ktm2rYT5TniDxj43Wy1ihjD59GW	400
		138eoqfNcEdeU9EG9CKfAxnYYz62uHRNrA	5000
		1Cq9sucCmX7M82JDm6qYpgk7C3RYZYQC22	2500
		16WvoYoAdPRja4g5SnKxiXmGxXKTj41toS	3300
		1LkukeTemkYDxKXxkTRit6XpTVuApnw31V	11000
		138eoqfNcEdeU9EG9CKfAxnYYz62uHRNrA	290
28.05.2010	2500	138eoqfNcEdeU9EG9CKfAxnYYz62uHRNrA	2500
09.06.2010	3600	16WvoYoAdPRja4g5SnKxiXmGxXKTj41toS	100
		138eoqfNcEdeU9EG9CKfAxnYYz62uHRNrA	3500
18.06.2010	5000	1LkukeTemkYDxKXxkTRit6XpTVuApnw31V	3700
		1DZFcB4AnHcabWnkTH4TYNqyVxUbe96n1w	300
		1Mru9STd941rgyEH8UvPrJBaJVr1kHbkp8	1000
19.06.2010	400	1CxpRFocvZ3xfGxDXM4T2Nb2PncB1vpu5q	50
		1HeotPnZVRbxGYtzWVo4s1FBZBqvGNqEqA	50
		1BnExE2TotsZQbiiE51MvUb1pyTGohzu7V	50
		16W39xn2MF4VtWw7xGUDGCDSUVytoULeF7	50
		15t65tSsRiDU63HzBYoo6FiQxejpst8fay	50
		14rXZuGJWnDmL8UbNQu2p4WLTsQtmU668o	50
		1H63ptHa99fTzx2pqbD4vRSGibMPKHBerw	50
		1JN9Qqizr8bSB9sjxrTgNVbpRj8hAVWEff	50
24.06.2010	3700	16WvoYoAdPRja4g5SnKxiXmGxXKTj41toS	400
		16WvoYoAdPRja4g5SnKxiXmGxXKTj41toS	150
		1GEECfBjkeUMCf3TNWCHvXZKKjnjjra7tC	3000
		16WvoYoAdPRja4g5SnKxiXmGxXKTj41toS	150
25.06.2010	3050	138eoqfNcEdeU9EG9CKfAxnYYz62uHRNrA	3000
		17ZC7FP7xe9SpBSiEx26CYQ3tw6u3ZEtB1	50
30.06.2010	295	1oxKqNXthUtE19NcWAihWg7peK95bMRQ9	50
		1EA8vHtfmFuRYMWfSBraiknBCPC4wWTYnb	50
		1NmfSbHC1q9S3Ww1ApvrvJruW5P3dTcWYC	50
		114o8MsUzJn7grKKo1woghmGc6wQAs58U2	50
		12PLHUQ2p56QX6Ht312q1WmZCFykuiGTyF	50
		14iQundB43KkLeuZG72nUch1UTUutTR1xS	45

If you have rubbed your eyes well and your mind is not affected seriously by all the alcohol you drank while reading the previous sections, look at the table above:

1. The wallets of people transferring money repeat

2. The first transaction dated 19 May 2010 to the tune of BTC10 was carried out by someone very close to this exchange. Perhaps, it was done to check the wallet. Perhaps, not. Here is

the address of the sender - 16RcAV7PN6QS3MaRtSEy3YbBfztA1DUxr.

For convenience's sake (or for you to finally express a desire to shoot yourself because of all this information), I systematized all the "investors" of the exchange into the following table:

Owners	Senders	Sent	%
THEYMOS	1LkukeTemkYDxKXxkTRit6XpTVuApnw31V	14700	87,68%
	138eoqfNcEdeU9EG9CKfAxnYYz62uHRNrA	14290	
	16WvoYoAdPRja4g5SnKxiXmGxXKTj41toS	4100	
	1Cq9sucCmX7M82JDm6qYpgk7C3RYZYQC22	2500	
	153wkZ3Ktm2rYT5TniDxj43Wy1ihjD59GW	400	
	Total	35990	
"Shahrazad"	1GEECfBJkeUMCf3TNWCHvXZKKjnjjra7tC	3000	7,31%
"Noname"	1Mru9STd941rgyEH8UvPrJBaJVr1kHbkp8	1000	2,44%
	1DZFcB4AnHcabWnkTH4TYNqyVxUbe96n1w	300	0,73%
	114o8MsUzJn7grKKo1woghmGc6wQAs58U2	50	0,12%
	12PLHUQ2p56QX6Ht312q1WmZCFykuiGTyF	50	0,12%
	14rXZuGJWnDmL8UbNQu2p4WLTsQtmU668o	50	0,12%
	15t65tSsRiDU63HzBYoo6FiQxejpst8fay	50	0,12%
	16W39xn2MF4VtWw7xGUDGCDSUVytoULeF7	50	0,12%
	17ZC7FP7xe9SpBSiEx26CYQ3tw6u3ZEtB1	50	0,12%
	1BnExE2TotsZQbiiE51MvUb1pyTGohzu7V	50	0,12%
	1CxpRFocvZ3xfGxDXM4T2Nb2PncB1vpu5q	50	0,12%
	1EA8vHtfmFuRYMWfSBraiknBCPC4wWTYnb	50	0,12%
	1H63ptHa99fTzx2pqbD4vRSGibMPKHBerw	50	0,12%
	1HeotPnZVRbxGYtzWVo4s1FBZBqvGNqEqA	50	0,12%
	1JN9Qqizr8bSB9sjxrTgNVbpRj8hAVWEff	50	0,12%
	1NmfSbHC1q9S3Ww1ApvrvJruW5P3dTcWYC	50	0,12%
	1oxKqNXthUtE19NcWAihWg7peK95bMRQ9	50	0,12%
	14iQundB43KkLeuZG72nUch1UTUutTR1xS	45	0,11%
"Wikipedia"/Founder	16RcAV7PN6QS3MaRtSEy3YbBfztA1DUxr	10	0,02%

Have you noticed something interesting here?

Have another look, bro.

Nothing? How's that? Everything is pretty clear!

Well, okay, here you have:

- "Wikipedia" / Founder transferred BTC 10 from the wallet 16RcAV7PN6QS3MaRtSEy3YbBfztA1DUxr, which we have already mentioned

- Over 80% of all the money was transferred by Theymos from a group of wallets associated with Bitcointalk
- Slightly over 7% of the money was transferred from a wallet called "Shahrazad" (1GEECfBjkeUMCf3TNWCHvXZKKjnjjra7tC);
- Slightly over 2% of the money was transferred from a wallet, the owner of which I did not find
- Slightly over 2% of the money was transferred from a group of BTC 50 wallets. I assume those were the first miners, who decided to invest their first mined capital in MtGOX: (

WIKI

Bro, sit tight. Now you will understand what Wikipedia has to do with this stuff.

So, back in 2014, there was a project (now it is not active) called "Blockchain Inspector." The purpose of this project was quite transparent (and interesting to my mind): it analyzed all transactions in the network using artificial intelligence. Thanks to this article (*https://goo.gl/LLba7a*), I learned that artificial intelligence also worked on two wallets of the investors in MtGOX. Another thing I found out is that the wallet, which created MtGOX, transferred money to Wikimedia Commons.

Rule 3

IF a Bitcoin address makes a transaction to a well-known foundation (like Wikipedia) THEN create a relationship "made a donation" to the foundation.

Existing data : The database contains an entity named "Wikipedia" which owns the address "16RCdSYjvj6PpCcbAWVzoArQaYVz3Tf5W4". We also know that "Wikipedia" is a foundation.

```
//-- Declaration of the rule.
ACTION& BitTransRule3 = NewRule(BitTransRule3Callback);

//-- Variables declaration.
CONCEPT& A = AddVariable(*CONCEPTS::BITADDRESS);
CONCEPT& B = AddVariable(*CONCEPTS::BITADDRESS);
CONCEPT& Foundation = AddVariable(*CONCEPTS::FOUNDATION);

//-- IF <A, InBitTransaction, Actor(BitTransRule3)> AND <B, InBitTransaction, Target(BitTransRule3)>
//--    AND <Foundation, Own, B>
AddGoal(BitTransRule3, A, *ACTIONS::INBITTRANSACTION, ACTIONS::GetActor(BitTransRule3) );
AddGoal(BitTransRule3, B, *ACTIONS::INBITTRANSACTION, ACTIONS::GetTarget(BitTransRule3) );
AddGoal(BitTransRule3, Foundation, *ACTIONS::OWN, B);

//-- THEN <A, Donation, Foundation>
AddEffect(BitTransRule3, A, *ACTIONS::DONATION, Foundation);
```

Rule 3 source code

So, this guy made a donation to Wikipedia, and then calmly invested the first BTC 10 in MtGOX. Those bitcoins were mined on 26 April 2010:

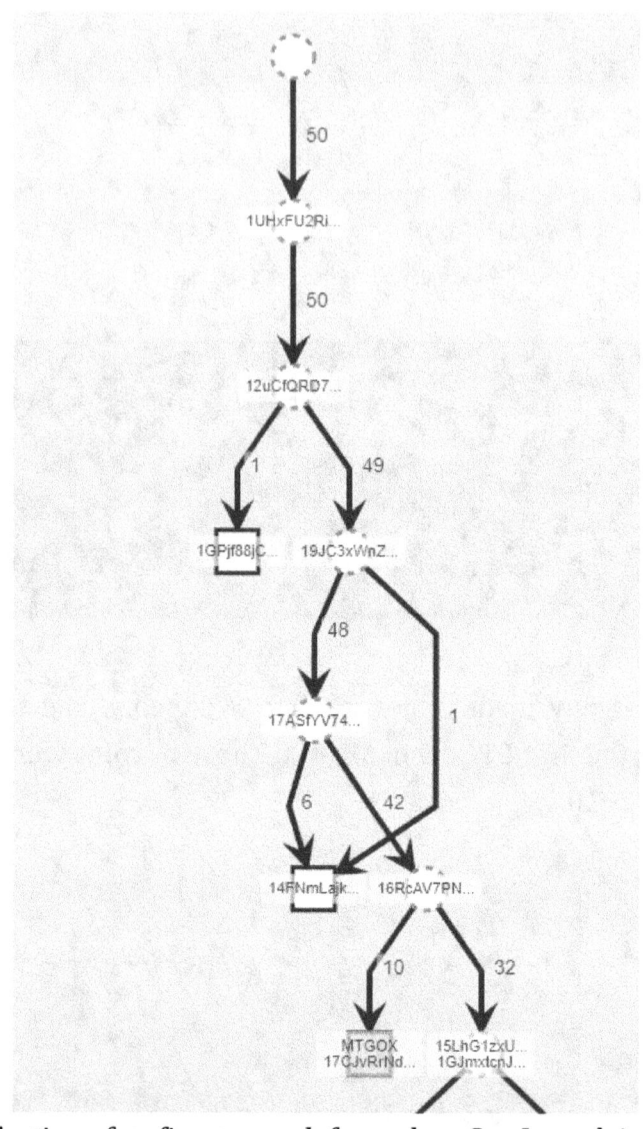

Now it's time for figures and formulas. So, I read in this article (*https://goo.gl/MZe1sp*) that a mediocre computer could mine X blocks a day back in 2010 using this formula:

(2271696 * 86400) / (4294967296 * N) = X blocks of BTC 50, where N is complexity.

The table from Bitcoin Wiki (*https://goo.gl/cRUkKz*) shows that the complexity was 11 on 26 April 2010. So, now we can calculate how many bitcoins a computer could mine per day:

(2271696 * 86400) / (4294967296 * 11) = 4 blocks of BTC 50.

What does it mean? It means that any of the first Bitcoin miners could be a patron. I failed to establish the specific name. If you ever find out who this man is, let me know, friend.

SHAHRAZAD

Dude, if you are reading these lines now, you have probably recovered from the previous investigation. Hot tears of frustration no longer roll down your cheeks, and faith - faith in a bright future of cryptocurrency - springs in your heart again. Don't become limp, pull yourself up, turn on quiet relaxing music, say, the Master of Puppets by Metallica, and read on.

So, my attention was attracted by another article on this site (*https://goo.gl/8gsCLS*). It offers the analysis of the Shahrazad wallet made by the artificial intelligence

1GEECfBjkeUMCf3TNWCHvXZKKjnjjra7tC.

Rule 1

IF an address (A) makes regular money transfer to another address (B) owned by an entity that is a restaurant THEN A's owner country = B's owner country.

Existing data : The database contains an entity named "Shahrzad" which owns the address "1GEECfBjkeUMCf3TNWCHvXZKKjnjjra7tC". We also know that "Shahrzad" is a restaurant located in Iran.

```
//-- Declaration of the rule. Takes as input a function that computes the rule's effects believes
//-- according to the unified goals.
ACTION& BitTransRule1 = NewRule(BitTransRule1Callback);

//-- Variables declaration. A variable has a type e.g. A is of type BITADDRESS.
//-- L is of type something that is a target of a GEO_POS action
CONCEPT& L = AddVariable(ACTIONS::GetTarget(*ACTIONS::GEO_POS));
CONCEPT& A = AddVariable(*CONCEPTS::BITADDRESS);
CONCEPT& B = AddVariable(*CONCEPTS::BITADDRESS);
CONCEPT& P = AddVariable(*CONCEPTS::LEGAL_PERSON);

//-- IF <A, InBitTransaction, Actor(BitTransRule1)> AND <B, InBitTransaction, Target(BitTransRule1)>
//-- AND <B, GeoPos, L> AND <P, Own, B>
AddGoal(BitTransRule1, A, *ACTIONS::INBITTRANSACTION, ACTIONS::GetActor(BitTransRule1));
AddGoal(BitTransRule1, B, *ACTIONS::INBITTRANSACTION, ACTIONS::GetTarget(BitTransRule1));
AddGoal(BitTransRule1, B, *ACTIONS::GEO_POS, L);
AddGoal(BitTransRule1, P, *ACTIONS::OWN, B);

//-- THEN <A, GeoPos, L>
AddEffect(BitTransRule1, A, *ACTIONS::GEO_POS, L);
```

Rule 1 source code

Why do I call this wallet "Shahrazad"? The fact is that its owner left the "Shahrazad" tag on the blockchain. He indicated it when creating a wallet. Another question arises. What is or who is "Shahrazad"? Do you think this is the main character of some oriental fairytale? Not at all. The Shahrazad is one of the most luxurious restaurants (*https://goo.gl/6Ae5t6*) in ... Iran. Iran, Carl!!!

The article, the link to which I cited above, says that transactions from this wallet were made to Iran. To make sure of this, I went to Blockseer and saw the following:

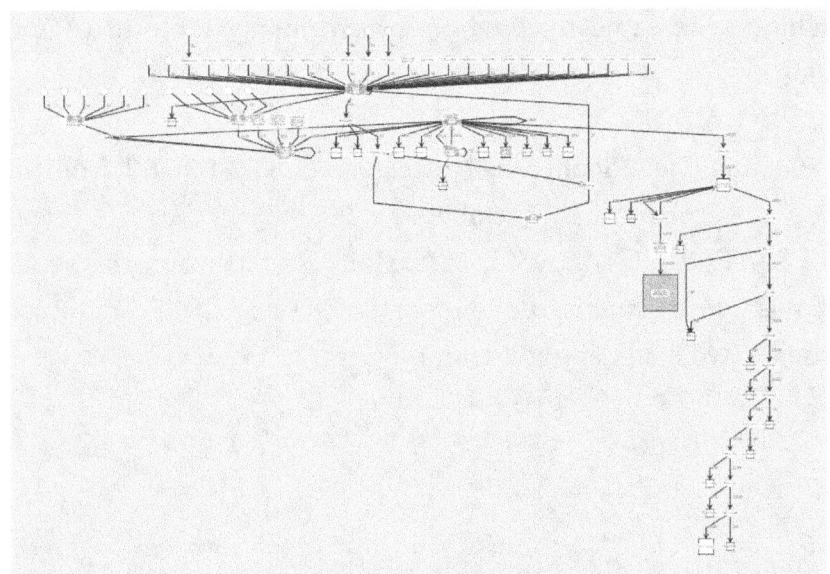

And here we should highlight three important points:

1. GOX.

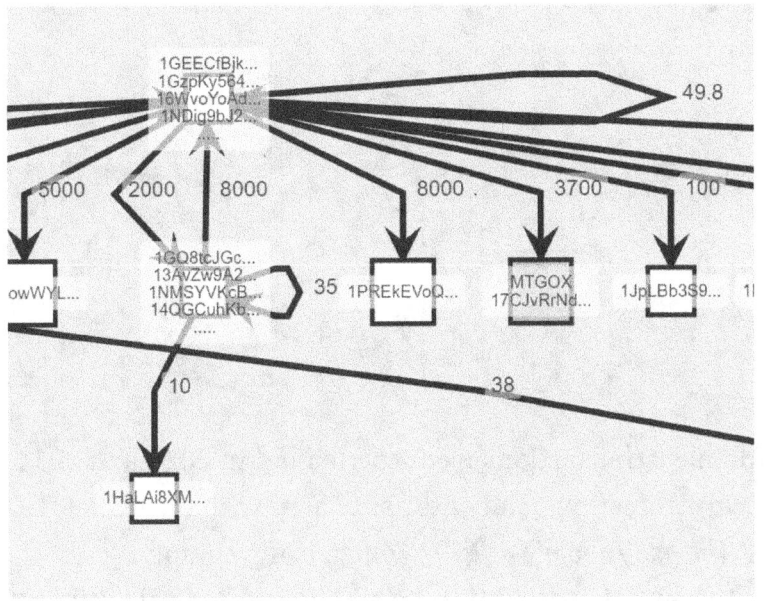

This is the same transaction I have in my table of GOX's "investors."

2. NOT A GOX.

Just imagine: "Shahrazad" transferred BTC 80,000 from own and related wallets to a wallet 1LUPDXYf9XD9Ee1AqCuM3gZCA3ZMKgTcgw. From this wallet, bitcoins were transferred either to "NOT A GOX" or Satoshi's carousel (we'll talk about it later).

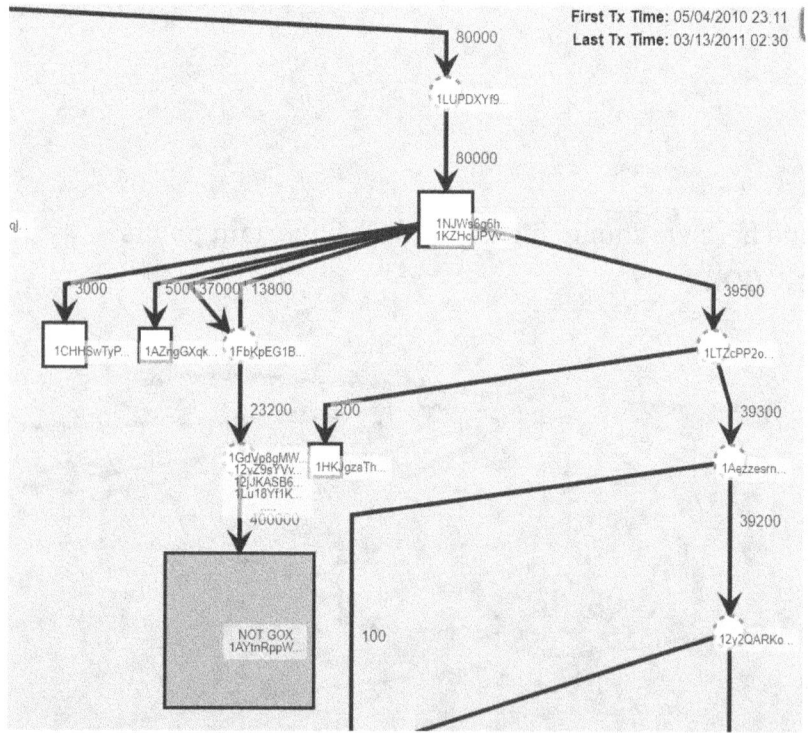

All these transactions were carried out in 2010 and 2011.

Two interesting points are associated with the wallet "NOT A GOX" (*https://goo.gl/kaJRUr*), which is now empty:

1. It is mentioned on Bitcointalk (https://goo.gl/zWXCkN) as being involved in the theft of funds from MtGOX, namely, it is

considered to be the gateway for withdrawal of stolen BTC 400,000. The analysis of its transactions on blockseer.com has indirect evidence of these claims.

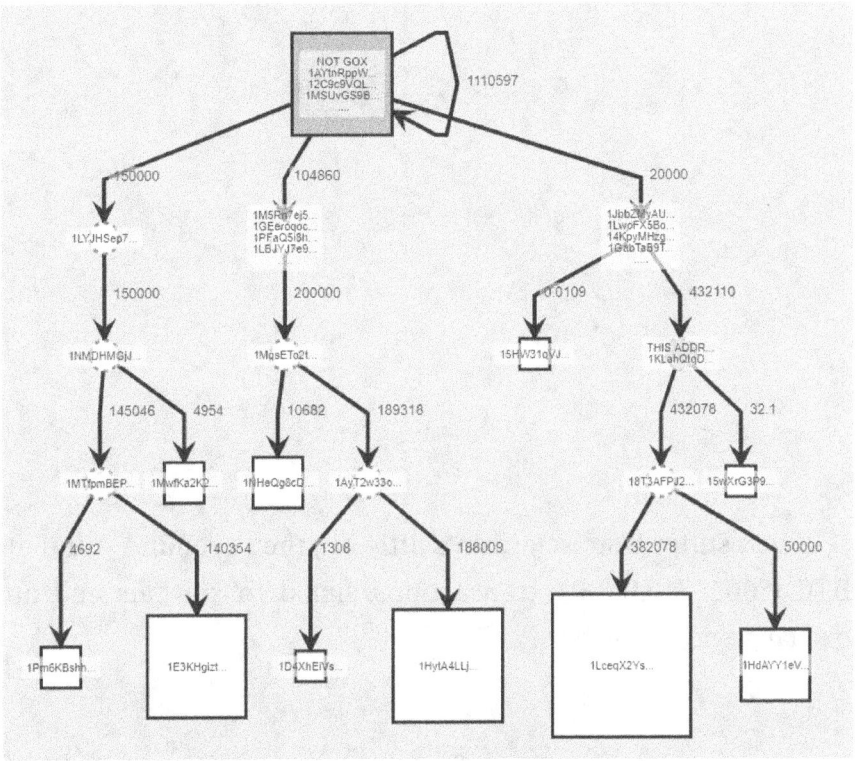

Afterward, these bitcoins were divided into small lots and transferred to different addresses. If you have a desire to contemplate all the final addresses of stolen bitcoins, someone had the trouble to provide them here https://www.cryptoground.com/mtgox-cold-wallet-monitor/.

2. The wallet "NOT A GOX" is the recipient of the microtransactions we have already mentioned. Look carefully and you will understand everything:

If you suffer from sclerosis a little bit, then I remind you that BTC 0.001 / 0.00001 transactions signal to start or end an exchange bot algorithm.

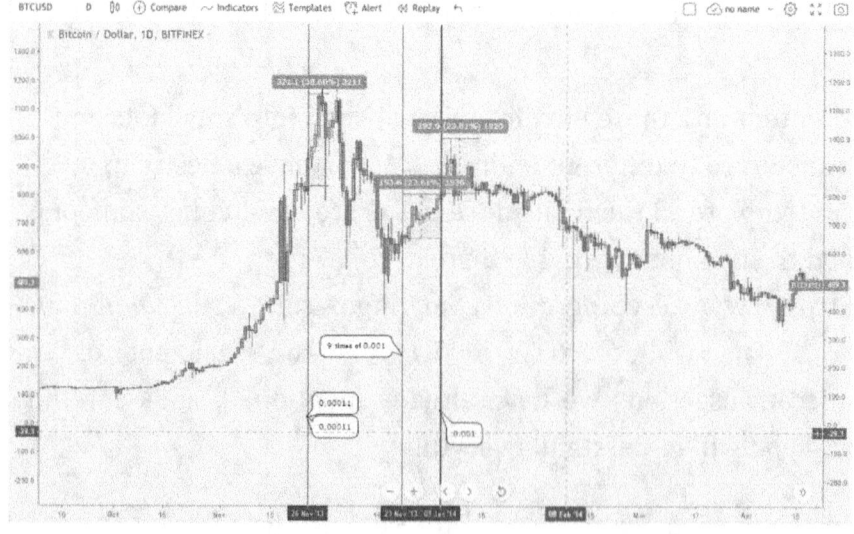

If to consider BTC 0.00011 transactions, they were made to the already empty "NOT A GOX" wallet (BTC 4 000 000 had already been withdrawn from there) from the 1QDTBF1Rynqfm1fhdFyNkhYeofxMcuqKDc wallet. If you open this wallet, you will see that it also received the microtransactions from "ENJOY" and "SOCHI" wallets we talked about in the previous section.

I also rummaged in the transactions of another group of wallets that transferred BTC 0.001 to "NOT A GOX" and found out the following carousel:

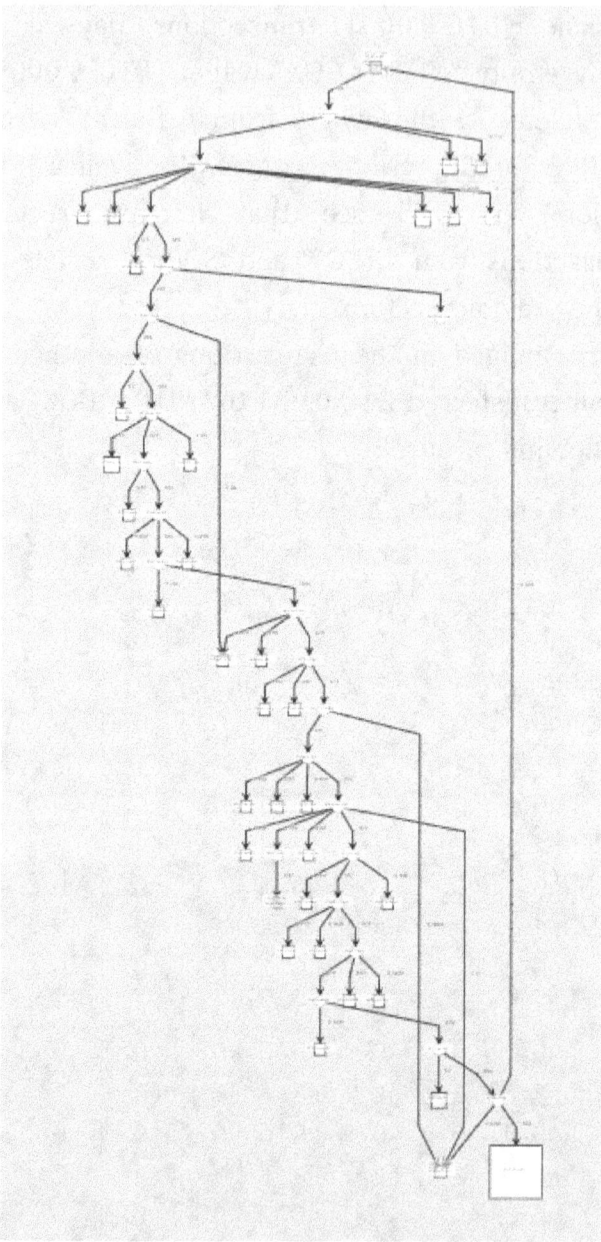

"NOT A GOX" is on the bottom left.

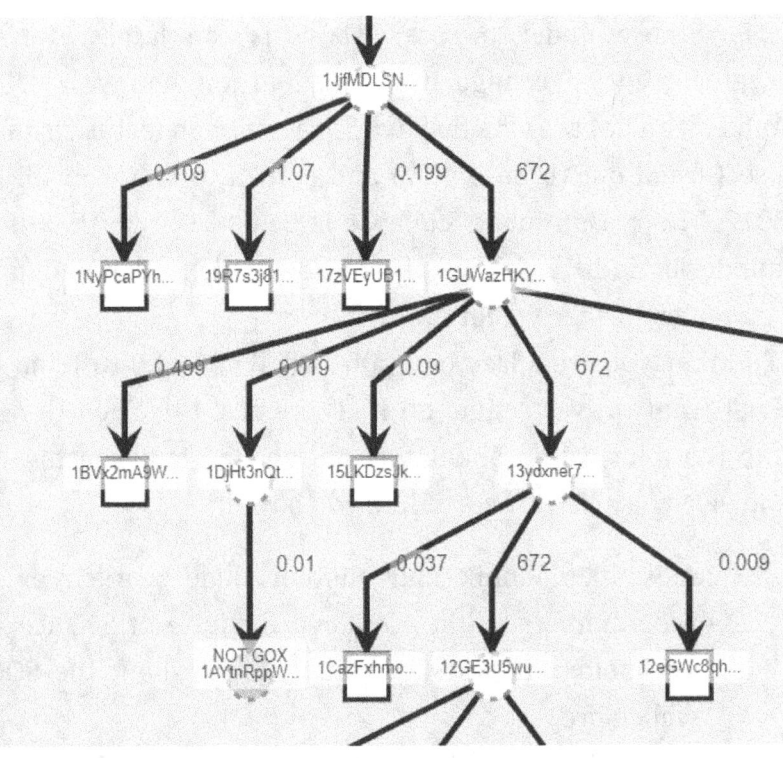

The carousel starts from btc-e.com (on the very top).

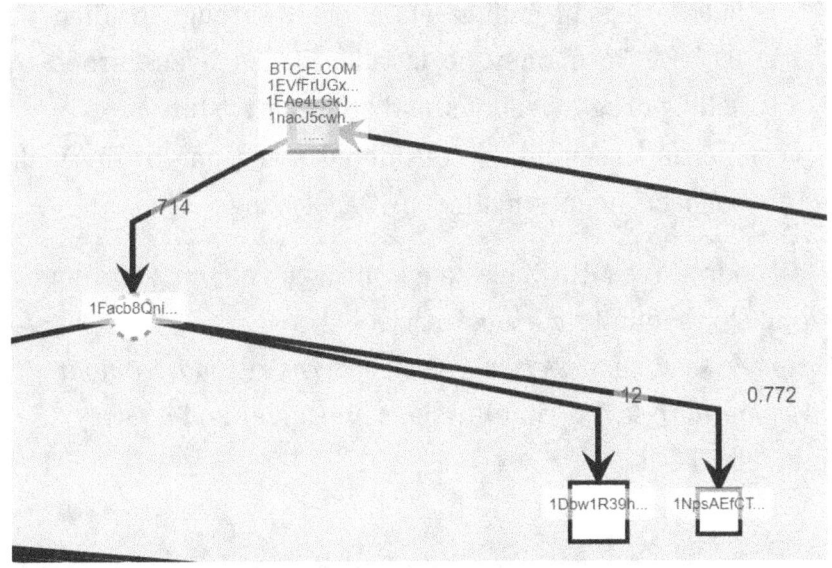

For those under a rock: BTC-E is the largest Russian cryptocurrency exchange. It has much in common with MtGOX. And I mean not the way they work). A common feature is that it also turned out to be a scam and ceased to work on 25 July 2017. The reason for its collapse is believed to be the money laundering in favor of one of its leaders, Alexander Vinnik (do you remember the wallet "SOCHI"?)

I know you are a lazy one (after all, I'm right, bro:) and you don't want to waste time on it. Therefore, I decided to delve into the information about this Alexander Vinnik on the web and give you a brief report. Here you have it:

- Alexander Vinnik and another dude worked as the programmers at the Skolkovo Institute of Science and Technology in Russia (do not forget about the SOCHI wallet, bro)
- The US authorities indicted Alexander Vinnik for laundering $4 billion via Bitcoin through trading on BTC-E. The money he laundered had been earned by selling drugs, weapons, and other nasty stuff
- Alexander Vinnik is considered to be one of the main suspects in hacking the MtGOX exchange.

Of course, the MtGOX exchange shrugged off our Alexander Vinnik, but I found a curious article (*https://www.coindesk.com/btc-e-concerns-russian-criminal-investigation*) saying that Russians Alexander and Aleksey founded BTC-E.

Cap it all, here is an article, or rather a report (https://goo.gl/hSH8qR) of the WizSec Japanese crypto security company, which proves the connection between Alexander Vinnik and hacking of MtGOX. You may read about the entire exchange hacking algorithm. Here's a map (https://wizsec.jp/images/theft_flow.svg) of movement of stolen dough from MtGOX. BTC-E is also mentioned.

3. Carousel of Satoshi Nakamoto

As you remember we have highlighted three points about the stolen money from MtGOX. So, the third "cell" where a part of the stolen money was transferred to is a so-called Satoshi's carousel.

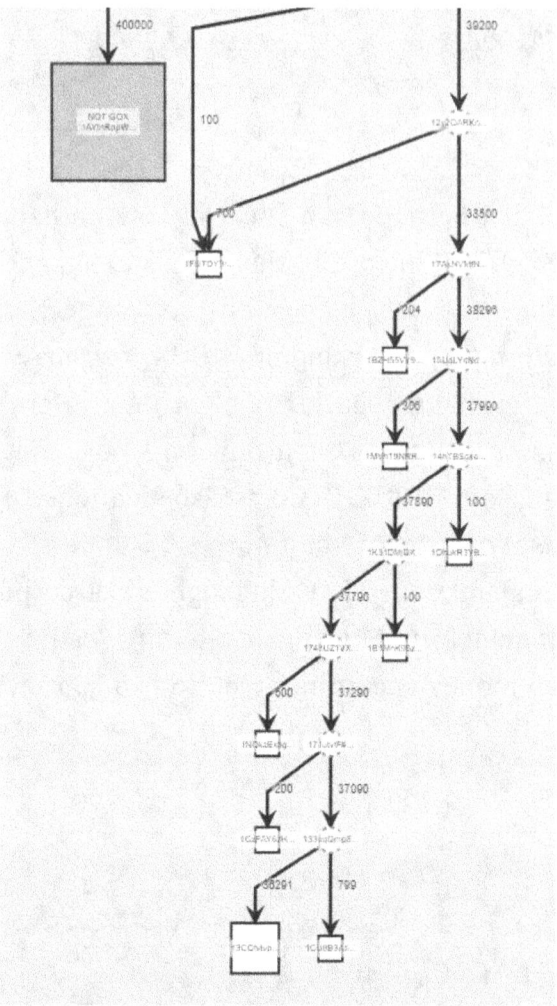

Of course, I started to examine this carousel on blockchain.com. The first wallet was 13CCfvtvppQnFtQxE12sNufVa9j4WNm3v2. The investigation led me to the wallet 17TZNT8CBPzUPDfKTXC25RQHrW6M2q6kRo, it still holds BTC 2,995. As part of the carousel, 204 bitcoins were transferred from this wallet to the wallet 1PCM4gvyAua6ZidxzUSARDCvtT4qUK4G7G in 2017.

I continued my research of the carousel in a similar way, but then it became harder as the carousel started to "pinch off" BTC 1-0.5 each turn. In the end, this path led me to the wallet 1JG4BAHYriwhDfzaPPLgg3NJkSDQ5vyUxk, which has been storing BTC 65 of this carousel since November 2017.

In short, this subsection happened to be interesting and just as tedious, so I suggest summarizing it:

- Alexander Vinnik hacked MtGOX exchange
- He got help "from the inside" of the exchange, perhaps, from his partner Aleksey. What do you think?

Now a few words about the Shahrazad wallet:

- This wallet was at the origins of the MtGOX exchange. Perhaps, it even had access to its internals
- BTC 80,000 of "erroneous double spending" were transferred to this wallet due to a "crooked" algorithm of MtGOX's hot wallet
- This wallet formed the assets of another wallet, namely NOT A GOX. A total sum of assets on these wallets is BTC 400,000, which is a multiple of BTC 40,000 from the "crooked" algorithm.

Guys from MtGOX

Before we start to gossip about the guys from MtGOX (LOL), let's recall the history of its creation a little bit. So, at first, the company was engaged in game cards trading, and famous Mark Karpeles emerged only in March 2011, when the exchange was sold to his Japanese company TIBANNE Co., Ltd. There was a couple of months to go until the arrival of our beloved Alexander Vinnik.

What do we know about the TIBANNE Co. Ltd? I can say only two things:

- The company's official website does not work
- I've found out information (*https://bitcointalk.org/index.php?topic=110356.0*) on Bitcointalk that in 2012 one dude was set to find the real address of this company. However, he found neither the office nor the employees. Perhaps, the company never existed?

But, damn, this world is so beautiful and the opportunities offered by the Internet are so wonderful as they strengthen our capabilities in the investigation enormously! So, I dug out on the Internet the business plan of MtGOX for 2014-2017. The top management of the then largest cryptocurrency exchange is represented in this good-sized plan by just a few words:

- CEO Mark Karpeles (*https://www.linkedin.com/in/karpeles/*)
- Director for Development Gonzague Gay-Bouchery (*https://www.youtube.com/watch?v=Mn16YZZEf0*)

When these two guys were no longer able to hide the truth about the stolen bitcoins, the history of their stock exchange became public. They hit the headlines. After the scam had broken out, it was decided to establish the MtGOX supervisory board. The board was appointed by a Japanese regulator when TIBANNE filed a formal bankruptcy petition. The board included CEO and founder of the Kraken cryptocurrency exchange Jesse Powell and chairman of the board of creditors (the supervisory board) Nobuyuki Kobayashi. In addition, many deceived traders, who dreamed to get their money back, became the board members. Feel sorry for those folks.

To sum up. Having read this endless section, you can easily twist your index finger at a temple and say I am cuckoo. However, can all these facts be just a mere coincidence? I do not think so! I hope you agree with me.

Come on, I'll unscramble it for you. We have only 8 points. Read them and go to bed. This mess in the market should be properly thought through:

1. The first investments in MtGOX were made by donators of Bitcointalk and Theymos

2. The very first donor of MtGOX was one of the early miners, who even made donations to Wikipedia

3. Another donor was a Shahrazad from Iran, who got many bitcoins after the exchange had been hacked

4. Alexander Vinnik is (most likely) the one, who managed to hack the exchange. He did that with the help of his partner and laundered the dough through BTC-E

5. Alexander Vinnik's partner (perhaps, Shahrazad?) has not been disclosed. Maybe, he is eating delicious meals in the Iranian restaurant right now and has hiccups?

6. Alexander and his partner worked as programmers at the same office in Skolkovo

7. Against Vinnik's background, ENJOY and SOCHI wallets seem to be even more connected with NOT GOX wallet. I assume that they were managed by Russians who were also involved in BTC-E

8. So-called "carousels of Satoshi" again emerge in the blockchain pinching off money from a handsome and transferring to thousands of small wallets followed by splitting.

CHAPTER 4. THEYMOS

If you think the previous section was too long and tedious, then I don't even know if you should start reading this one? Hmm...

Maybe, we shouldn't damage your mind so much, because it will take not one or two pages of this book to figure the mess entitled "Theymos" out. It may seem like a real hell! If deep inside you still think you are a strong man (even if you are a lady, LOL), then be patient, take a cup of coffee (or glass of whiskey) and move on. I was typing for too long, take pity on my fingers and delve into this section)

Let's review: Theymos was the first administrator of Bitcointalk and spent all Bitcoin donations for the wrong purpose: he invested in MtGOX.

Our character, called Theymos, actually has a name, Michael Marquardt. You can read more information about him here (*https://goo.gl/5UinvW*). And here are his email addresses:

- theymos@mm.st
- theymos@gmail.com
- theymos@hotmail.com
- theymos@aol.com
- theymos@yahoo.com.

To get the following results of the investigation, I used only open network information. So, now I will give the basic links of all the Theymos wallets with each other and other members of the network.

If you examine the picture carefully, you can come to the following conclusions:

- theymos@mm.st is the main e-mail address of Mr. Theymos. Moreover, when sending messages, the dude used PGP encryption[7]
- The above email address was used to send messages to the following addresses: ian.maxwell@gmail.com, email@rylandtaylor-almanza.com, cjplooy@ultimatestunts.nl, frankf44@gmail.com, dfolkins@temple.edu, cdouble@mozilla.com, js9119@live.com

---

[7] **Pretty Good Privacy (PGP)** is an encryption program that provides cryptographic privacy and authentication for data communication. PGP is used for signing, encrypting, and decrypting texts, e-mails, files, directories, and whole disk partitions and to increase the security of e-mail communications.

- theymos@mm.st also corresponded with the address michael_m@mm.st. How did I define it? It's very simple! A trace (*https://goo.gl/dp7WYy*) of the exchange of PGP encryption keys remained on the web
- Our Theymos is also registered here (*https://www.flickr.com/photos/21584737@N07*), although he did not publish anything. Two his e-mail addresses point to the account on this site: theymos@gmail.com and theymos@yahoo.com
- And last but not least, the addresses theymos@mm.st and michael_m@mm.st (despite PGP) give us a link with a certain Michael Marquardt.

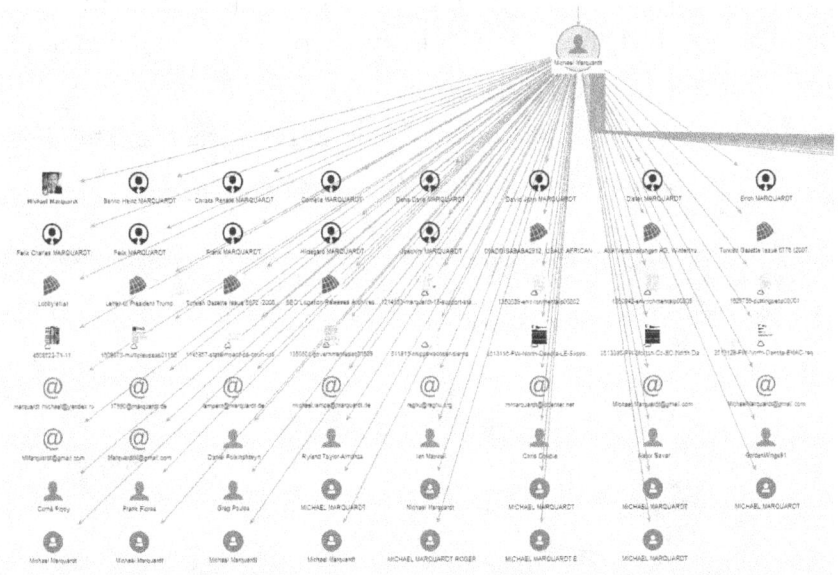

My further investigation leads me to a lawsuit involving the domain Bitcoin.org, where the U.S. Department of Justice identifies our Theymos as Michael Marquardt (*https://goo.gl/FcJK9v*).

The safeguards around Bitcoin.org allow Theymos to take over in an emergency, like if "Cobra was hit by a bus or something," he said. Theymos, who was identified as Michael Marquardt by the U.S. Justice Department in a 2014 subpoena in the case against Ulbricht, is against a change in ownership for Bitcoin.org.

"While domain names like Bitcoin.org are inherently centralized and therefore subject to at least some fallible humans, I find the idea of handing Bitcoin.org to some politicizable nonprofit organization to be very distasteful," Theymos wrote in an email. "In some sense, the whole point of Bitcoin and the cypherpunk movement from which it spawned was to escape politics."

Now I will share my conclusions with you. You may believe them or not (but I hope you'll believe, bro). So, I assume that our Theymos is a guy from Wisconsin (*https://pastebin.com/Wsua0hS7*). Find his address and telephone number (and even Skype) below (or click the link):

```
1.  Name: Michael Marquardt
2.  Emails: theymos@mm.st / theymos@gmail.com / theymos@hotmail.com / theymos@aol.com / theymos@yahoo.com
3.  Personal: michaelmarquardt@mm.st
4.  Phone: 920-358-0624
5.  Address: 1552 Park St
6.  City: Middleton
7.  State: Wisconsin
8.  Zip: 53562
9.  DOB: June 15, 1991
10. Domain: theymos.com
11. Skype: theymos1
12. Last 4: 7352
13. EXP: 01/16
14. SSN: xxx-xx-0179
15. Relatives: Laurie Marquardt
```

THEYMOS & MtGOX

Dude, right now I want to see your surprised face with bulging eyes (I am laughing now, ahahaha). I can imagine you asking how this cracky author established the identity of Theymos we are reading about from the very first page of the book. In short, you may not thank me, it's all for you, my dear reader :) Hold that I have already introduced you to Theymos, so let's go on.

So, we are lucky that someone was very careless on the network as now we have the following information for our investigation. On December 17, 2017, someone sent an email to theymos@mm.st . And imagine, an attachment, an 84-page pdf file, "fell out" of that letter.

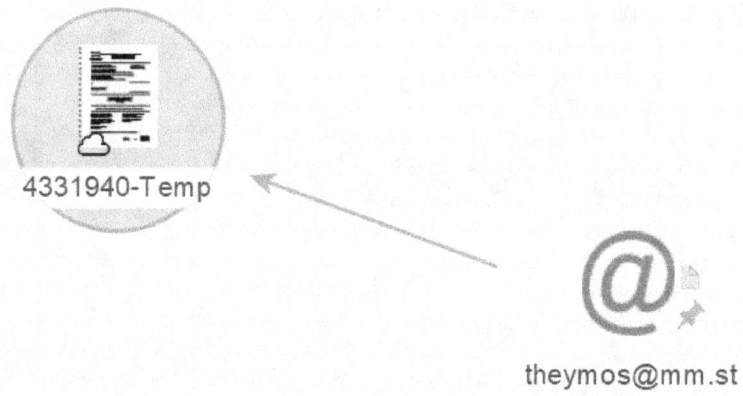

theymos@mm.st

To view this attachment, click here (*https://www.documentcloud.org/documents/4331940-Temp.html*).

For my lazy readers, who never follow my links and prefer to receive a brief report instead, I should say: the attachment in the letter contained case files of the sitting of the Supreme Court of Mississippi (*https://goo.gl/kof5km*) dated 17 December 2017. These case files reveal that a plaintiff (a family of doctors from Mississippi) lost $133 million or BTC 9,500 due to the MtGOX scam. They filed a lawsuit against MtGOX, TIBANNE KK (a legal entity of MtGOX), Jed McCaleb (who owned 12% of MtGOX), Mark Karpeles (owned 88% of MtGOX), MUTUM SIGULUM LLC, CODE COLLECTIVE LLC and a group of guys under the name of John Does.

Therefore, my friends, a connection between Mr. Marquardt and MtGOX is obvious again.

BEST FRIENDS OF THEYMOS

Thanks to the Internet, I revealed that our Theymos (Michael Marquardt) contacted such people:

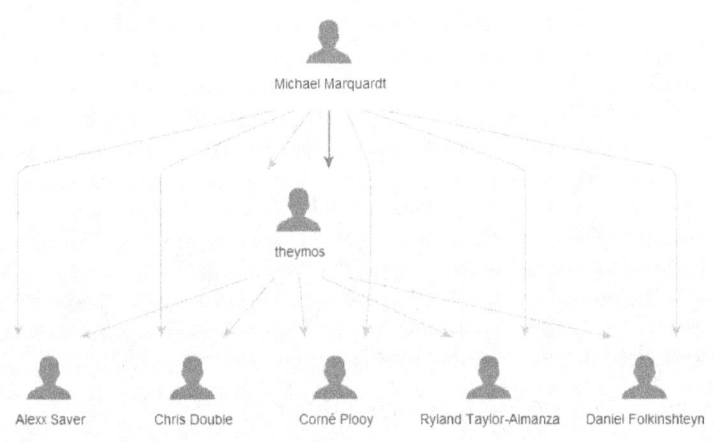

And now the most interesting part begins. We will consider each of them, from the smallest (I'm talking not about height now) to the biggest ones.

Chris Double. A completely odd man who knows everyone in the cryptocurrency community. But why? Maybe, he is an adept guitar player. God knows why the lumps mix with him.

Ryland Taylor-Almanza. This guy has a very interesting story. He sells medicines, his website (*http://rylandtaylor-almanza.com/*) is linked to Russian IP, registered on ".com", and the server address leads us to Cyprus (Limassol, Agios Fylaxeos 66 and Chr. Perevou 2, Kalia Court, off. 601). If you have tried to open his site and failed, do not rush to accuse me of lying. The fact is that this link really does not open, there is a redirect via a referral link to another online pharmacy. Here it is *big-pharmacy.com*.

Coorne Ploy. He is privy to German / Dutch OTC platform Bitonic.nl, where BTC 375,000 has been sold for the whole time of its existence.

The platform accepts bank payments and also has a cryptocurrency exchange. The interesting thing is that it also accepts the payments from SEPA. If you are familiar with the matter, you understand that there may be a lot of obscure money.

Daniel Folkenshteyn. He seems to be a very clever person. He has a PhD in Finance (*https://goo.gl/GHgiEC*), even works as an assistant professor at the Temple University in Philadelphia. He is also the author of many articles about Bitcoin (*https://goo.gl/piFrWG*). Do not be lazy and read at least some of them. In fact, the articles are very good, for example, about Bitcoin as a destroyer of the classical financial system, about cryptocurrency and Nasdaq, about possible applications of Bitcoin, etc. And again: all these articles have something very interesting and much in common, namely a similarity of writing style and subject matter with a book by Satoshi Nakamoto. Are you following?

NeoFutur. The analysis of correspondence of the latter dude, Theymos and other guys lead us to their relationship with a certain William Waisse (he is NeoFutur, *twitter.com/neofutur*). Here are the addresses: neofutur@ww7.be, wwaisse@neofutur.net, bitcoin.org@ww7.be. I hope the last e-mail address also helped you notice that this guy is mixed up with Bitcoin.org and Mark Karpeles.

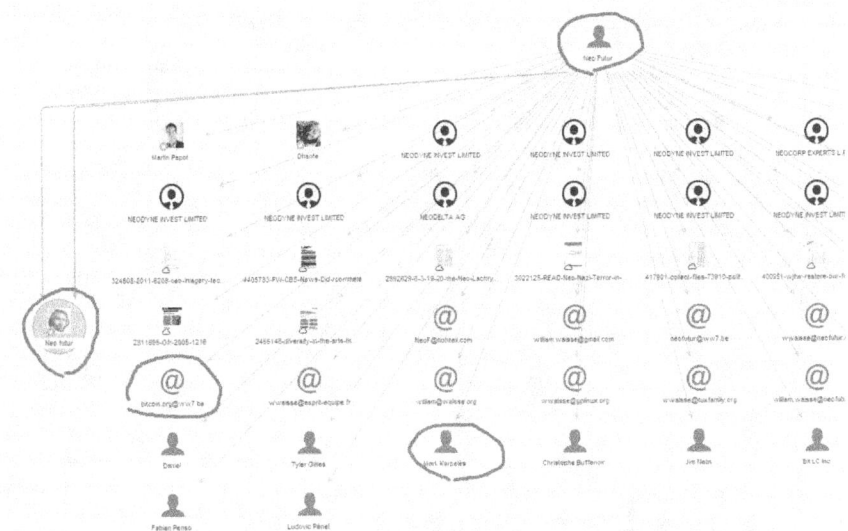

This dude also owns offshore legal entities:

NEODYNE INVEST LIMITED (Белиз) *https://goo.gl/UjHB5m*;

NEOCORP EXPERTS L.P. (Уэльс) - *https://goo.gl/d5pFHj*.

I suppose he could settle the matters at the edge of offshore fiat and Bitcoin.

And finally, no. 1 on our chart of Theymos' friends is Alexx Saver (*twitter.com/lzsaver*, SaverA@hotmail.com, AlexxS@gmail.com, ASaver@gmail.com). He is top dog, believe me. He has something to do with Namecoin Central and CENTRAL ELECTRONIC MARKET EXCHANGE, INC (*https://goo.gl/xh778T*).

And Russia emerges again. The leader of our chart is associated with a certain Kirill Temnenkov (KirillTemnenkov@gmail.com, KirillT@gmail.com), and he, in turn, ties into the exchange we have mentioned a little bit earlier - BTC-E. If this dude is such a super Bitcoin activist from Russia, maybe he is Aleksey, a Vinnik's partner?

Alexx Saver

@lzsaver

Bitcoin Activist

◎ Russia

▦ Joined June 2009

And now don't even ask me how I found the following facts. Bro, I understand you are dying to know, but I can't reveal all my sources. So, here you have three Bitcoin wallets of Alexx Saver:

Alexx Saver
+lzsaver

following ●

My Bitcoin address:
1EPNVhKEmk6eQJtpnkYJnk5yyMnGR2KbpZ
My OpenPGP fingerprint:
5099EB8C0F2E68C63B4ECBB9A9D0993E04143362

OTR Fingerprint:
D64C6A1F 707592EB C1B797F3 46870116 EA68A21D

-----BEGIN PGP SIGNED MESSAGE-----
Hash: SHA256

About
Bitcoin Community
Linux/Solaris user

AKA
lzsaver, lz, saver, isa

Contacts
Jabber: lzsaver@jabber.ru
Skype: lzsaver

Donation (bitcoin and namecoin addresses)
1lnux7eD8H13GrvBvdPiUbW7oSz8osgD8
NCxVfZLYzU1tpjZSwdRbu2F9S2bdyq2eoR

GPG fingerprint:
5099EB8C0F2E68C63B4ECBB9A9D0993E04143362

Let's look at the transactions of each on these wallets. The first one is 1EPNVhKEmk6eQJtpnkYJnk5yyMnGR2KbpZ. The last transaction on this wallet was carried out on 19 January 2011. The total number of transactions is two, while the total number of bitcoins received is 700. Let's follow these bitcoins via blockchain:

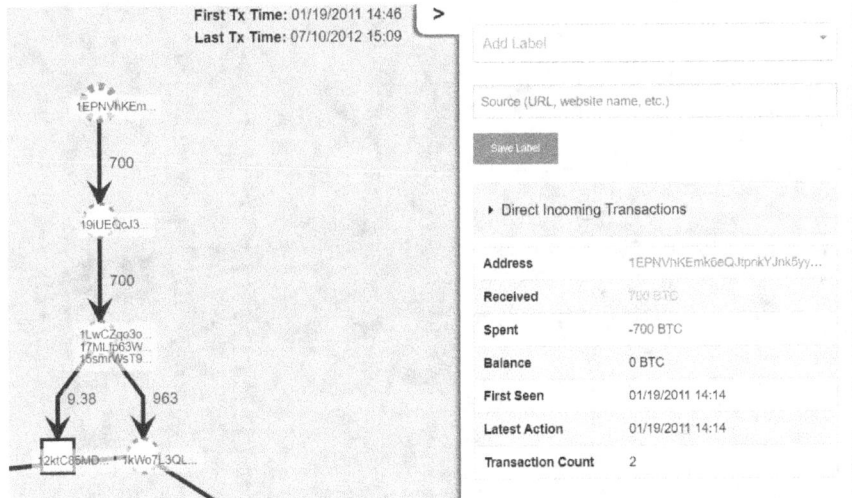

It's a starting point.

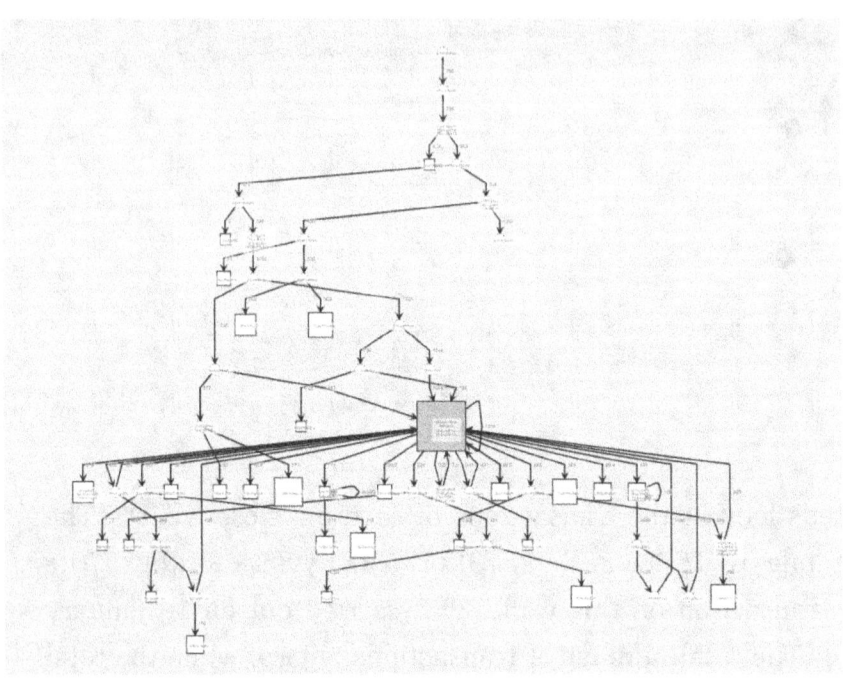

It's a path of coins.

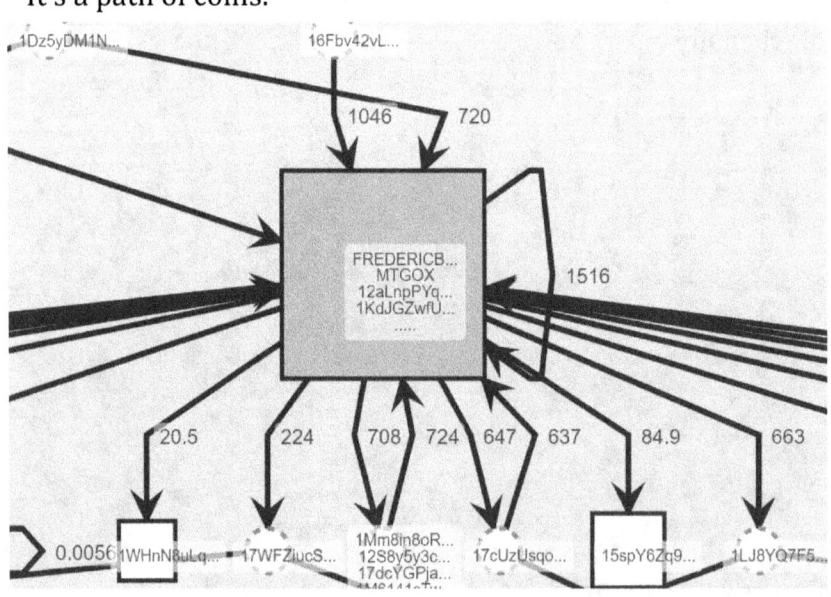

And here we have a destination. Curiously, the ultimate goal is the Frederic Bastiat MTGOX wallet!

Alex's second wallet is 1inux7eD8H13GrvBvdPjUbW7oSz8osgD8. The last transaction on this wallet was made on 7 March 2017.

And Alex's third wallet is 1inux6wWiTBsQwU3pPG856rSvPVi8evX4. I found it due to the similarity of names among the transactions on the wallet above. The last transaction on this wallet was made on 7 March 2017.

By the way, you can find a lot of recurring small transactions on the other two wallets. Do you remember what they mean?

And one more thing: I found that our Alex is one of the Bitmessage (*https://bitmessage.org/wiki/Main_Page*) developers (a free program for exchanging encrypted messages between two or more users). It is his relevant github repository (*https://github.com/lzsaver*).

HERE COMES JOHN DOES

You could not have such a bad memory to forget how the family of doctors was suing over the loss of big money from the scamed MtGOX. So, some other legal entities were on the case files. To complete the picture, I will tell you about them:

MUTUM SIGULUM LLC was a kind of gateway (*https://goo.gl/2wgPKn*) through which money was transferred to MtGOX.

CODE COLLECTIVE LLC is a company located in New York and managed by a professor of Chinese descent Wendy W Fok. She turns out to be an architect / designer *(https://twitter.com/WendyWFok/).* So what does this company do? It writes codes for neural networks and website designs. There is no direct connection between CODE COLLECTIVE and MtGOX, but it seems crooked to me. I do not rule out these guys made a site for MtGOX!

"John Does" is a name for yet unknown persons involved in the case. There are five such persons in the case of doctors v. MtGOX.

And now let's try to draw conclusions from all paranoid insanity I described in the present section. If you gather all these folks into one system, you'll get the following "tree of coincidence":

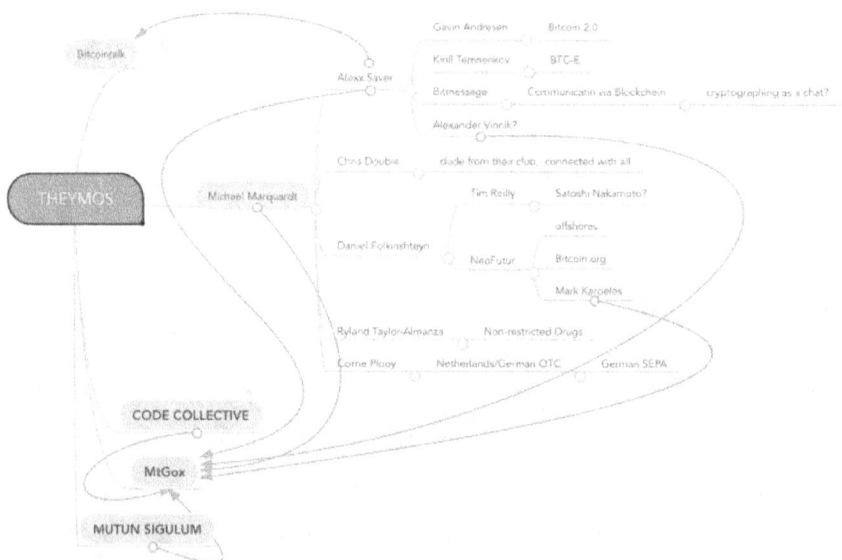

Theymos invested in MtGOX, was involved in the lawsuits on MtGOX case and in the Bitcoin.org case. Theymos is associated with Daniel Folkenshteyn (who is the author of many scientific works very similar to the books of Satoshi Nakamoto), and he, in turn, is mixed up with NeoFutur and through him ties into off-shores and Mark Karpeles.

Theymos is also believed to be mixed up with the European OTC branch with access to the banking sector and SEPA.

Alexx Saver (like Theymos) is one of the Bitcointalk administrators. He is friends with Kirill Temnenkov, who is associated with BTC-E. Let me remind you that Alexander Vinnik (the creator of BTC-E) had a colleague Aleksey, who could help him to hack MtGOX. Perhaps, he is our Alexx Saver?

The same Alex left traces in the blockchain, thanks to which we ended up with MtGOX, a certain Frederic Bastiat and microtransactions.

How do you like this puzzle? Do you want to shoot yourself? Me too! We have found a lot of information, but how are we going to systematize it?

CHAPTER 5. WHO ARE THE WHALES AND HOW TO STAND UP TO THEM?

I f you are already tired of the frequent repetition of the words like MtGOX, BTC-E, THEYMOS, and others, give a sigh of relief as I'm going to mention them less (or not to mention at all, we'll see). In fact, I still have plenty of evidence of microtransactions in the blockchain which serve as a kind of signals to raise or lower the Bitcoin price, but I will not lay all my cards on the table right now. I'm waiting for feedback from you, my dear reader (yes, from you), about this investigation and whether I should continue it. If this book resonates with you, I will update it (I've almost burst into tears from my words, LOL).

So, I dedicate this section to the whales. Not to those sweet creatures swimming in the ocean, but to the ugly and shifty ones living among us. Ugh. Perhaps, this section will finally destroy your faith in the bright future of cryptocurrency, but it's not my fault, bro.

So, if you decided that the whales in the cryptocurrency market are a certain John, Chris or Michael, then you are mistaken. It is the exchanges that are the whales in the cryptocurrency market. It turns out that you deal with these whales every day (Binance, Poloniex, Bittrex, Bitfinex and other trash), you visit them, but you do not know who they are. How come?

Auntie Wikipedia will tell you about each exchange, its creator, daily volumes, etc., and I pursue other goals.

Tell me please: have you wondered why 99.9% of altcoins can be sold or bought on the exchange only for Bitcoin? The answer is simple: it is easy to have a control lever for quotations (i.e., prices). Suppose you want to exchange some Dogecoin for fiat money, will you care about Bitcoin? Blast it all! You will make a direct exchange and won't give a rat's tail about Bitcoin price. However, if you want to buy chewing gum and you have only some kind of Siacoin in your crypto wallet, then you will have to buy Bitcoin first, then exchange it for fiat money, and only then you will be able to buy your chewing gum, damn!!! Get the picture of an insane situation we have been forced into?

Therefore, sure thing, all the movement in the market will continue to involve Bitcoin as otherwise (in case of introduction of direct pairs on the exchanges), the interest in Bitcoin will drop while the interest in fiat money will grow. For example, USDT will be much more profitable than Bitcoin. And what will the crowd do in this case? Sell Bitcoin in pursuit of fiat.

Only exchanges can give people direct pairs. And who the exchanges are? That's right, they are whales. So it becomes clear why we should not wait for pairs. Never (R.I.P.).

Now tell me one more thing: why do different states and various regulatory bodies (for example, the SEC) make constant attempts to somehow do harm to cryptocurrency exchanges? **And one more question**: why does every exchange in the stock market undergo the international licensing procedure obligatorily? If some stock exchange dares to violate a rule, especially regarding manipulations, an SEC officer will knock at its CEO's office door in a couple of minutes and say: "Leave the market, you are hosed."

The fact is that the guys working over there (in the state financial supervision!) understand perfectly well (obviously unlike you and me) all kinds of jiggery-pokery in the market and how it affects prices, traders and so on. That is why all the exchanges are taken under control.

Do not entertain illusions that the SEC controls the exchanges because it strives to protect my or your rights. They frankly do not care. But they do care for the hedge funds that invest in the cryptocurrencies fearing to face a new 2008 crisis on the stock market. The money of hedge funds are now not in the real world, but the virtual one (I'm talking about blockchain, just so you know).

And what is a blockchain? "Oh, here we go," you thought. Don't worry, bro, I want to touch upon another thing. Many people view blockchain as the universal salvation, where anonymity and absence of government control reigns. People have been living with this thought for many years, hoping that now no one interferes in their lives and they themselves rule in the blockchain. But the reality is that the rulers are still there.

Not the governments, but the whales rule. Therefore, they will continue to hinder the activity of the government agencies: to hide in offshore companies, relocate hostings, etc.

Here's the next question: the rich boys have already earned a lot of money, so why should they continue to manipulate the market? To answer this question, I suggest thinking about the following situation. Let's imagine you have $500 million (do you imagine?), you decided to buy Bitcoin for this money. If a Bitcoin price is $8,000, you will buy BTC 62,500. But you have two options:

- You can buy all the "market depths" on all the exchanges (and jack the Bitcoin price up to the moon)
- You can negotiate with the whales and enter the over-the-counter market, so you can buy Bitcoin without affecting its price.

I doubt you will not like the second option. Therefore, you get acquainted with large Bitcoin holders and start to bargain: one offers to buy coins at the exchange price, another one offers a 7% discount, and the third promises a discount of 8.5% but warns there will be a market drawdown first and later it will resume its natural course. You are interested in the last dude, it's logical. This is how your deal will look like: you pay your $500 million for BTC 68,306 at the rate of $8,000 and with an 8.5% discount (8,000–8.5% = 7,320).

Well done, bro, you made a very good deal. But have you wondered what happens at this moment to the dude who sold you Bitcoin? BTC 68,306 was taken from him at a price of $8,000 per one Bitcoin totaling $546,448,000. His loss is

$46.448 million. Despite this trying situation, this dude is not so hopeless because he is a whale, which means he has an exchange. And what about this exchange? There is a crowd of hamsters there! Do you understand me? He will invest about $3 million in the price dump, drop it by 8.5% (maybe even lower), buy up these coins at a low price and not only cover the losses but even make a profit.

Now you can once again ask yourself the abovementioned question (will these manipulations stop?) A person has no sense of proportion, regardless of nationality, religion, etc. If people can make money, they will do it. So my prophecy is: MANIPULATIONS WILL NEVER STOP.

And the last question, guys: what should we do in this foul situation? My answer is: to adapt to such a market.

Now I will reveal you the secret of secrets. If you benefit from it, then remember me at least sometimes with good blessings:)

So, you can use a bug in the blockchain, namely the open transaction statistics. Here is the link (*https://goo.gl/HmRhzG*) where you can find all the top Bitcoin wallets. Do you understand what you should do with this info? Look at the transactions and you will be able to forecast the upcoming market manipulations.

If getting closer to practice, then my advice is not to wait for new altcoin/fiat pairs (one or two may be added a year but at such a rate it will continue till the end of the world). All operations will continue to involve Bitcoin, and it will be further manipulated.

Some tips more:

- Always put stop orders on the exchange
- Do not buy a lot of altcoins, choose a small amount and trade them
- Trade actively when Bitcoin prices are flat
- Change for fiat if you feel something is wrong.

Those, who do not want to bother with trading, may try a long-term investment. It's a less nerve-racking business.

CHAPTER 6. USDT

Some cryptocurrency experts call 2019 the year of stablecoins[8]. Do you know what is it? It's a type of cryptocurrency tied to usual currency or commodity. Why are these stablecoins so cool and why are they believed to be in great demand? Mad volatility of Bitcoin and other cryptocurrencies just piss the dudes in the market off. What about you? This is how they want to solve the problem of inadequate price fluctuations when today you are a millionaire, and tomorrow you are a beggar.

Why do I say this? I try to explain why I chose the USDT as the topic of the last (a bonus one, if you like) section. First of all, the USDT is a stablecoin, and second, this business called "USDT" is quite shady.

Are you ready for a new investigation? Let's go!

I'm going to start with the curious stuff:

- If you do not know yet, Tether Limited and Bitfinex are different offices only by the letter of the law, while actually, it is one and the same thing;

---

[8] **Stablecoins** are cryptocurrencies designed to minimize the effects of price volatility.

To minimize volatility the value of a stablecoin can be pegged to a currency, or to exchange traded commodities (such as precious metals or industrial metals). Stablecoins backed by currencies or commodities directly are said to be centralized, whereas those leveraging other cryptocurrencies are referred to as decentralized.

- After Bitfinex delisted USDT from the Binance exchange (despite the possibility to make arbitration of price difference between BTC / USD and BTC / USDT), it gained a pretty sum of money through fraud with USDT and fiat dollar.

Whitepaper

Of course, we should start to delve into this topic from its very origins, namely the Whitepaper USDT (*https://goo.gl/fFfea1*). There you can find a scheme according to which the USDT should circulate:

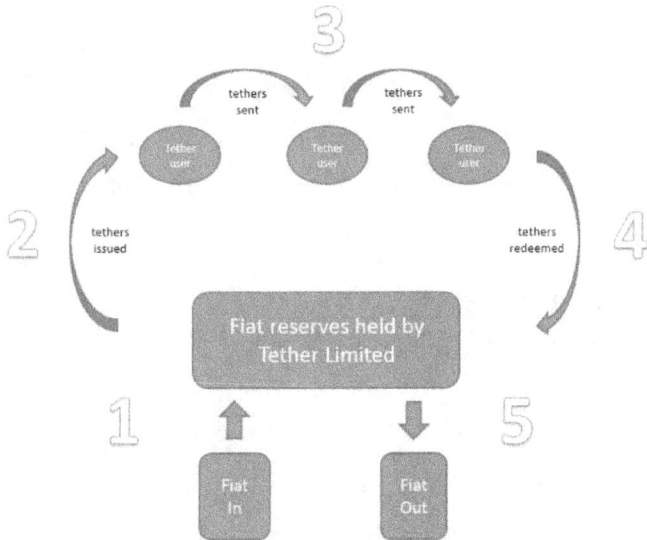

If to present this information in form of a bullet list, it looks like this:

- Fiat is deposited on a Tether Limited bank account
- Tether disburses a loan equivalent to the deposit's amount (if you deposit real $100, you get virtual USDT 100)

- The received USDT is transferred to a person who deposited fiat

- Well, if you need fiat, then you deposit your USDT in Tether Limited and get a sum of fiat money equivalent to USDT. The most interesting thing is that the USDT returned to Tether Treasury is completely destroyed

- If you need a new fiat deposit, new USDT tokens are created for this purpose

- Another way to get USDT (except Tether Limited) is to trade, this money can also be withdrawn in form of fiat.

Everything seems pretty simple and decent at first glance. But this impression is deceiving, my friend. Aren't you disturbed by a point about the destruction of the returned USDT? The fact is that the USDT Treasury is not a "repository", the tokens sent there must be subsequently destroyed since sending USDT to Treasury is treated as cashing USDT.

Main USDT wallets

The main wallets of this entity are:

- USDT "printer" and the main issuer wallet 3MbYQMMmSkC3AgWkj9FMo5LsPTW1zBTwXL

- New "Treasury" or Tether Treasury 1NTMakcgVwQpMdGxRQnFKyb3G1FAJysSfz

- Old "Treasury" or Tether Treasury 2 3BbDtxBSjgfTRxaBUgR2JACWRukLKtZdiQ

- Bitfinex wallet 1KYiKJEfdJtap9QX2v9BXJMpz2SfU4pgZw

- Binance wallet No.1
  1KQ4DHSvR4zN5ZEQS9SfV71DK5rwm529KG
- Binance wallet No.2
  1FoWyxwPXuj4C6abqwhjDWdz6D4PZgYRjA
- Huobi wallet No.1
  1LAnF8h3qMGx3TSwNUHVneBZUEpwE4gu3D
- Huobi wallet No.2
  168o1kqNquEJeR9vosUB5fw4eAwcVAgh8P
- Bittrex wallet
  1DUb2YYbQA1jjaNYzVXLZ7ZioEhLXtbUru
- Poloniex wallet
  1Po1oWkD2LmodfkBYiAktwh76vkF93LKnh.

I summarized the balances of all these major USDT wallets in a table (but do not forget that the figures were true at the time of writing this chapter):

Wallet	Amount of USDT	USDT/USD rate	Amount is USD
"Printer" USDT	0,00		0,00
Tether Treasury (old)	0,00		0,00
Tether Treasury (new)	966 678 763,48		953 573 499,48
Bitfinex Wallet	36 208 812,56		35 717 929,69
Binance #1 Wallet	593 591 062,91	0,986443	585 543 748,87
Binance #2 Wallet	100 942 372,64		99 573 896,89
Huobi #1 Wallet	93 274 462,28		92 009 940,39
Huobi #2 Wallet	42 272 049,09		41 698 966,92
Bittrex Wallet	129 418 522,53		127 663 995,62
Poloniex #1 Wallet	3 310 444,30		3 265 564,61
Total	**1 965 696 489,79**		**1 939 047 542,48**
Tether Treasury from total	966 678 763,48	49,18%	953 573 499,48
On exchanges from total	999 017 726,31	50,82%	985 474 042,99

All USDT are distributed in a very interesting manner, don't you see? It must have happened by chance! Yeah, I tell you, it's a coincidence)

Here's the data on USDT at this point in time (you can check at the latest info on coinmarketcap.com).

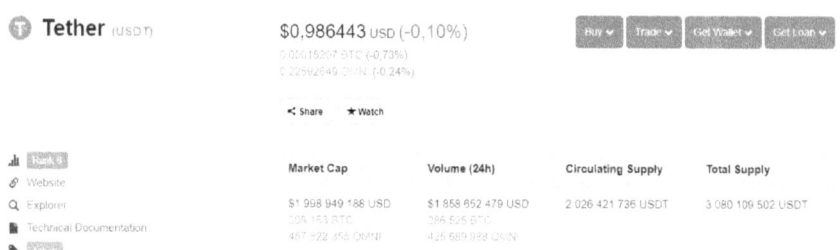

If we set ourselves the task of putting two "pictures" above together, then we get such global USDT bookkeeping:

Location	Amount of USDT	USDT/USD rate	Amount in USD	%
Total amount of USDT	3 080 109 502,00		3 038 352 457,48	100,00%
Tether Limited Treasury	966 678 763,48		953 573 499,48	31,38%
Frozen USDT	35 949 980,00		35 462 606,12	1,17%
Destroyed USDT	30 000 000,00	0,986443	29 593 290,00	0,97%
Out of turnover	21 059 022,52		20 773 525,35	0,68%
Amount in circulation	2 026 421 736,00		1 998 949 536,53	65,79%
On the exchanges	999 017 726,31		985 474 042,99	32,43%
On the wallets of network users & other exchanges	1 027 404 009,69		1 013 475 493,53	33,36%

The difference in the data on the total amount of USDT and their amount in circulation, which is indicated on the site coinmarketcap.com, is obvious. The difference consists of USDT 966.68 million in the Treasury (frozen and destroyed USDT) and USDT 21 million out of turnover (and I do not even know what kind of group it is).

If not to analyze this scheme, it looks nice: one third is in the Treasury, one third is one the exchanges from the list (shown in the main wallets), and another third is on the wallets of network users and other exchanges. To date, 31.38% of the printed USDT has been withdrawn from circulation. I think it is the only precedent in the history of the whole existence of this entity called "USDT".

Moreover, since September 1, 2018, such transfers from Bitfinex to Treasury and vice versa have been noticed:

Transfers	Amount of USDT
Transfer from Bitfinex to USDT-Treasury	885 718 600,00
Transfer from USDT-Treasury to Bitfinex	-150 000 000,00
Total	735 718 600,00

Thus, out of USDT 966.68 million in the Treasury, at least USDT 735.72 million came from Bitfinex, being about 76% of the total volume stored there.

PRINTING PRESS

I am sure that each of you at least once in life came up with the analogy between the work of the USDT network and the printing press. That is true for me as well) The wallet 3MbYQMMmSkC3AgWkj9FMo5LsPTW1zBTwXL performs this function in this entity. It is this wallet that prints and destroys USDT tokens.

The last transaction from this wallet (I remind you: the last one at the time of writing this book) was carried out on 29 September 2018. A total of 100 bucks were transferred. At the same time, the last batch of USDT tokens was "printed" on 25 June 2018.

A point is that this wallet not only prints tokens but destroys them as well (the process of destruction is called "Revoke

Property Tokens"). Thus, if we see the destruction, we can get information on the withdrawal of fiat from the Tether Limited bank accounts.

It turns out that it only once (31 January 2018) destroyed USDT 30 million over the entire existence of this "printing press."

Tokens were destroyed only once, but they have been "frozen" several times:

FREEZE USDT	
Date	Amount of USDT
23.10.2018	960 000,00
23.10.2018	1 060 000,00
09.10.2018	2 039 980,00
24.09.2018	940 000,00
21.11.2017	30 950 000,00
Total	35 949 980,00

If my memory doesn't fail me, the rumors went in September 2018 that vulnerability was found on the USDT network. The hype subsided and we quickly forgot about everything, but all the "frozen" tokens in 2018 were reflected in the USDT network several times, and this resembles a "double spend", doesn't it?

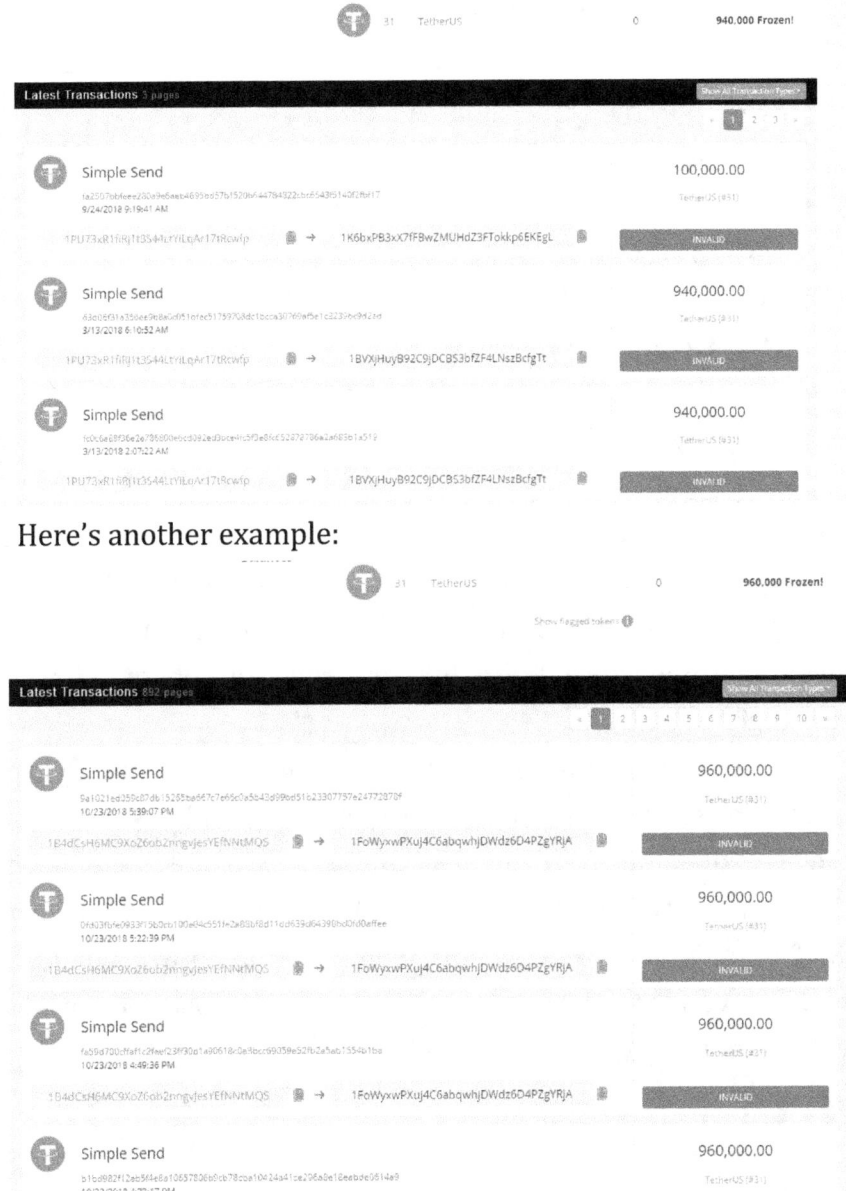

Here's another example:

And here you have a list of the wallets with "frozen" tokens:

- 30 950 000 USDT (no double spend, *https://goo.gl/1D6Z4h*)
- 940 000 USDT (potential double spend, *https://goo.gl/qrDTzV*)
- 2 039 980 USDT (potential double spend, *https://goo.gl/gPnb9J*)
- 1 060 000 USDT (potential double spend, *https://goo.gl/UiVhES*)
- 960 000 USDT (potential double spend, *https://goo.gl/UiVhES*)

It's very strange that only 1% of USDT (30 million from the total treasury of 3 billion) was actually withdrawn, cashed and destroyed on the USDT network before, during, and after the Bitcoin pump worth USD 20,000. Is it true that nobody withdrew anything?

It is also strange that the USDT code was allegedly hacked, and at the same time, there was a "freeze" of a total of USDT 4.999,980 (the freezing did not involve USD 30.950,000 that is not accompanied by strange transactions). It turns out that they froze USDT 5 million and then rumors went that the network had been hacked. I wonder if the vulnerability has already been removed or, perhaps, nothing was hacked at all?

Making money without Bitcoin
When investigating this topic, another issue drew my attention: how could the guys from Treasury + Bitfinex + Binance + team

make money on USDT delisting from the Binance exchange and without taking into account the possibility of Bitcoin arbitration between BTC / USD and BTC / USDT.

Let's look at the USDT / USD price chart on the Kraken exchange:

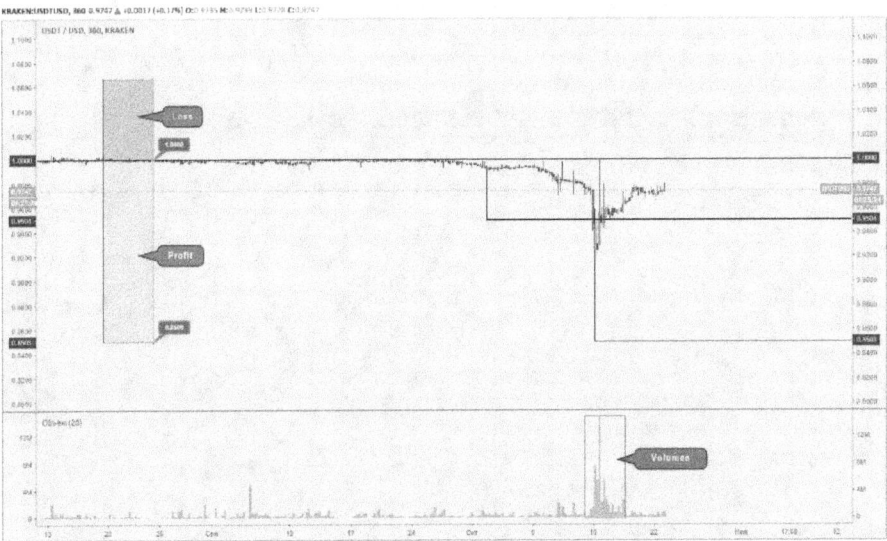

And now let's recall a little bit what I wrote above: according to the Whitepaper and USDT circulation scheme, you need to have some USDT in Tether Treasure to get some fiat dollars on your bank account. At the same time, these USDT must be destroyed through Revoke Property Tokens.

Now I switch your attention to the volumes (indicated by number 2) during the fall after delisting (figure 1):

Tether Charts

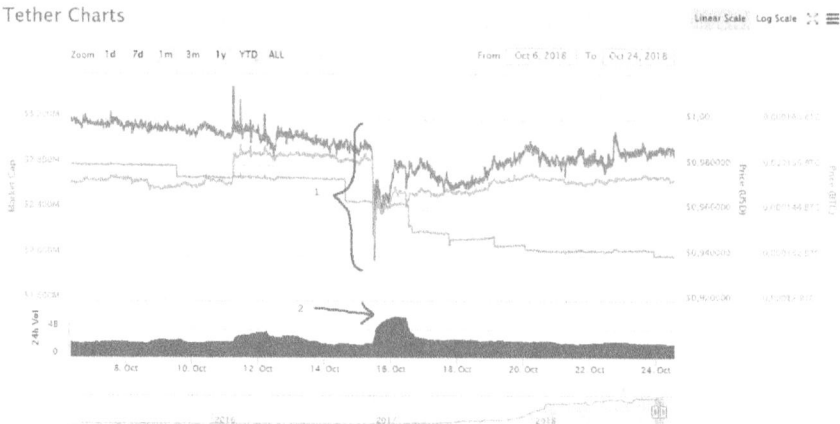

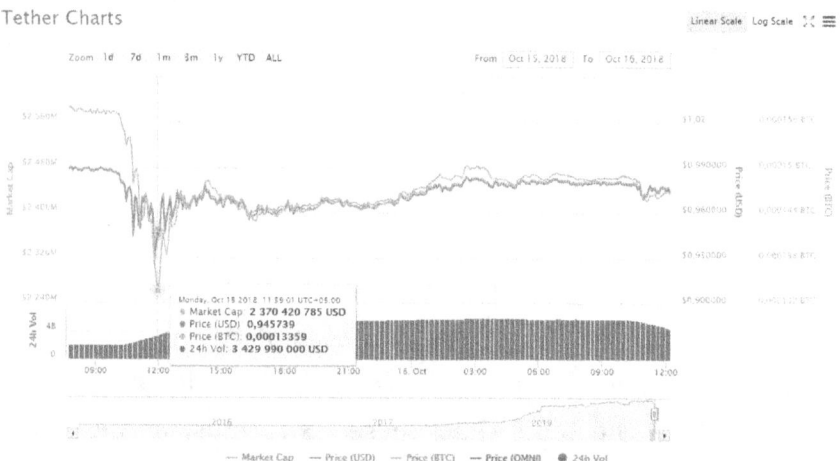

Now look at the latest history of USDT in figures:

Date	Open*	High	Low	Close**	Volume	Market Cap
Oct 23, 2018	0,984913	0,990374	0,982528	0,987962	2 111 740 000	2 045 094 991
Oct 22, 2018	0,985726	0,995210	0,976333	0,983998	2 213 350 000	2 046 782 394
Oct 21, 2018	0,984348	0,988854	0,974997	0,983548	2 188 330 000	2 043 920 962
Oct 20, 2018	0,988241	0,990877	0,977601	0,983631	2 094 040 000	2 052 004 385
Oct 19, 2018	0,981291	0,989284	0,978021	0,987712	2 322 570 000	2 096 639 263
Oct 18, 2018	0,972522	0,985084	0,967321	0,980858	2 485 030 000	2 145 792 803
Oct 17, 2018	0,977078	0,978690	0,966323	0,971225	2 559 210 000	2 204 699 680
Oct 16, 2018	0,979243	0,985358	0,969406	0,975152	2 585 550 000	2 454 395 592
Oct 15, 2018	0,993084	0,993084	0,925284	0,980138	5 891 700 000	2 489 087 954
Oct 14, 2018	0,987869	0,995905	0,984209	0,989570	2 008 170 000	2 673 590 361
Oct 13, 2018	0,995036	0,995455	0,984940	0,988046	1 961 540 000	2 692 987 558
Oct 12, 2018	0,998704	0,998704	0,983870	0,994102	2 962 380 000	2 702 915 064
Oct 11, 2018	0,992934	1,02	0,987252	0,993026	3 772 600 000	2 687 298 290
Oct 10, 2018	0,995332	1,00	0,990803	0,993502	2 295 300 000	2 693 788 327

If you slightly alter the historical data, you can get the following:

Date	Open price	High price	Low price	Close price	Average price(1)	Volume	Capitalization	Market Cap DELTA (2)	Potential profit (3)
Oct 20, 2018	0,99	0,99	0,98	0,98	0,99	2 094 040 000,00	2 052 004 385,00	-34 634 878,00	31 122 669,50
Oct 19, 2018	0,98	0,99	0,98	0,99	0,98	2 322 570 000,00	2 086 639 263,00	-59 153 540,00	36 982 282,11
Oct 18, 2018	0,97	0,99	0,97	0,98	0,98	2 485 030 000,00	2 145 792 803,00	-58 906 877,00	58 531 775,36
Oct 17, 2018	0,98	0,98	0,97	0,97	0,97	2 559 210 000,00	2 204 699 680,00	-249 695 912,00	68 523 399,91
Oct 16, 2018	0,98	0,99	0,97	0,98	0,98	2 585 550 000,00	2 454 395 592,00	-34 692 362,00	58 718 486,89
Oct 15, 2018	0,99	0,99	0,93	0,98	0,97	5 891 700 000,00	2 489 087 954,00	-184 502 407,00	159 679 799,25
Oct 14, 2018	0,99	1,00	0,98	0,99	0,99	2 008 170 000,00	2 673 590 361,00	-19 397 197,00	21 310 198,00
Oct 13, 2018	1,00	1,00	0,98	0,99	0,99	1 961 540 000,00	2 692 987 558,00		
Total	0,98	0,99	0,97	0,98	0,98	21 917 810 000,00	18 799 197 596,00	-640 983 173,00	434 868 611,02

How did I make these calculations? First, I stroke an average price having compared the Open / High / Low / Close day candlesticks. Second, I calculated the delta (change) in the amount of USDT in the market. And third, I calculated "potential profit" if one buys USDT on the cheap and sell for $1 through Tether Limited, as the Whitepaper says.

It turned out that it is possible to withdraw $434.9 million in net profit from the entire market, but the amount of USDT decreased to the tune of about 641 million.

Here are the transfers from Bitfinex to Tether Treasury from October 14 to October 20, 2018, totaling USD 680 million:

Date	Transfers of USDT from Bitfinex to Tether Treasury
14.10.2018	200 000 000,00
16.10.2018	250 000 000,00
17.10.2018	50 000 000,00
18.10.2018	50 000 000,00
19.10.2018	80 000 000,00
20.10.2018	50 000 000,00
	680 000 000,00

Personally, I do not understand why there is such a discrepancy: 680 million and 641 million. Whatever there is something more interesting. If we assume that the net profit should be calculated from the returned 680 million, then we are talking about (680.000,000 / 0.98) – 680.000,000 = 13.900,000 USD.

The figure looks very nice, I agree. But I am sure that the guys earned much more money.

Conclusions

I can say only one thing: you, my dear reader, as always have the right to believe my investigation or burn a book (or throw your e-book reader away, LOL). Although my calculations are approximate, the main fact cannot be rejected - some guys made a lot of money on the pump of all cryptocurrencies to USDT. And this sum is not USD 13.9 million.

In my opinion, Bitfinex and Binance masterminded that performance. And if everything is clear with Bitfinex, two things point to Binance: a) USDT delisting rumors went from Binance; b) Binance had already got TrueUSD (TUSD), which no one paid attention to until October 2018.

Now, let's get together our conclusions and thoughts:

- As Whitepaper USDT says, new tokens are printed only upon receipt of a fiat deposit on a bank account and are destroyed when fiat is withdrawn from a bank account

- Fiat deposits and withdrawals took place in fact

- Meanwhile, Revoke Property Tokens (or destruction) for all the time has affected only USDT 30 million (it's a very small sum, bro). I am sure that the sum of destroyed USDT is not equal to the sum of fiat withdrawn from the bank accounts of Tether Limited

- I assume that all USDT tokens, which should have been destroyed after fiat withdrawal, were returned to Bitfinex. That is, this money is backed by nothing, entailing the crooked nature of a USDT "entity", scandals involving auditors, etc;

- Whale Bitfinex used this freebee money to buy Bitcoin. Nobody found out about this, because all the centralized exchanges (is there another type, bro?) work under an algorithm implying that nobody can find out what is happening inside the exchange itself. But the USDT becomes necessary when you sell Bitcoin for USDT and then you want to withdraw this USDT

- But what did Bitfinex whale end up with? USDT "dummies" spread in the market, which means a task appeared to collect them back. And when it should be done? Of course, at the end of our favorite triangle (technical analysis experts will understand), which started from 20,000. That's when "delisting" happened

• To date, about USDT 967 million have been returned to Tether Treasury (and I am sure much more will be returned). It could also affect the market, yeah?

In a word, it is most likely to be only a part of a large strategy (if I may call this conspiracy a "strategy"). At first, the guys organized a Bitcoin pump at the expense of USDT, and then, using the "revoked" USDT which was not supported by fiat, bought Bitcoin at the lowest price.

What to expect next? I think we should expect a new wave of hype because the triangle is nearly over, the Bitcoin lows cannot last forever and the guys are trying to handle a situation with the help of unsupported USDT. Therefore, let's get ready to growth triggered by news about sorts of ETF, Bakkt, etc.

CONCLUSION

You know, buddy, I can well imagine how much you have liked (or hated) me after reading this book. I really hope that it is the insight into the whole "decentralization" nature of our dear cryptocurrency world - not into the genius or, perhaps, the madness of some authors – that prompts you to put my book in a frame and hang it on a wall (or give it to the dogs).

The book, which you are holding now in your hands, is not just a set of letters on several dozen pages. It is a booklet for every cryptocurrency investor. No, dude, this book should not dissuade you from holding. This book also should not cease your attempts to trade successfully. You're welcome to work and make money! In fact, the book aims not to unmask a group of bad guys but just to open the investor's eyes before he or she decides to sell the property for the sake of buying cryptocurrency. Investors should know what they get tied up in.

It does not matter whether we have succeeded in finding Satoshi Nakamoto in the course of our super secret investigation or not. It does not even matter whether we have found the link between currently popular Bitfinex exchange and already scammed MtGOX. Even less important is the relationship between a Russian (a certain Alexander Vinnik) and Iranian restaurant Shahrazad. The connection between microtransactions in the network and a sharp spike in coin price is absolutely not important. Why aren't USDT tokens destroyed? Never mind!

"Hold on a sec! – you may tell me bewildered – Why on earth have I read all this nonsense if everything in the book is not important?"

And I will ask you a rhetorical question: do you know why this investigation involving those characters taken all together counts for nothing? It's because the only person of importance is you, my dear reader. Only your thoughts, your goals, and your intentions are essential. All the letters in this book are no more than just a spice in your dish. It is not a crucial ingredient, but still, it gives a zest.

For all the time of its existence, cryptocurrency has experienced various stages of development, including rapid prosperity and a dizzying fall. However, while such dudes as you and I (LOL) are in the market, it will not go west but will continue to work and, perhaps, will even surprise everybody on this earth shortly.

In a word, I want you to come to understand that it is not my investigation or misbehavior of some people that matters but your faith in the market. If you know clearly the whole situation around and are willing to continue working (and dodging also), you will definitely get what you want from the cryptocurrency business.

Many thanks for devoting a part of your precious life to sort of a scribe I am and reading my book till the end. If I see a sincere interest in such investigations from my readers, I am ready to knock off another piece of work. I will keep killing your faith in the bright future of technology, invented by not so mysterious Satoshi Nakamoto :)

Take care, bro, and see you soon!

About The Author

Alan T. Norman is a proud, savvy, and ethical hacker from San Francisco City. After receiving a Bachelor's of Science at Stanford University. Alan now works for a mid-size Informational Technology Firm in the heart of SFC. He aspires to work for the United States government as a security hacker, but also loves teaching others about the future of technology. Alan firmly believes that the future will heavily rely on computer "geeks" for both security and the successes of companies and future jobs alike. In his spare time, he loves to analyze and scrutinize everything about the game of basketball.

Mastering Bitcoin for Starters

(http://geni.us/mastering-bitcoin)

Cryptocurrency Investing Bible

(http://geni.us/crypto-investing)

Blockchain Technology Explained

http://geni.us/blockchain-book

CRYPTOTRADING PRO: Trade for a living with time-tested strategies, tools and risk management techniques. A contemporary guide from the beginner to the pro

http://geni.us/cryptotrading

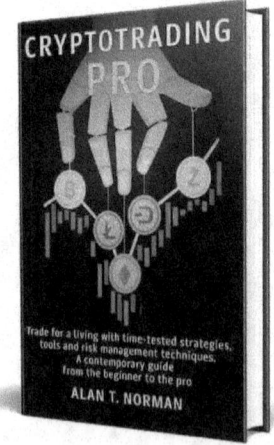

Hacking: Computer Hacking Beginners Guide

(http://geni.us/hacking-book)

Hacking: How to Make Your Own Keylogger in C++ Programming Language

http://geni.us/hacking-keylogger

HACKED: Kali Linux and Wireless Hacking Ultimate Guide

(http://geni.us/hacked)

One Last Thing...

DID YOU ENJOY THE BOOK?

IF SO, THEN LET ME KNOW BY LEAVING A REVIEW ON AMAZON! Reviews are the lifeblood of independent authors. I would appreciate even a few words and rating if that's all you have time for

IF YOU DID NOT LIKE THIS BOOK, THEN PLEASE TELL ME! Email me at alannormanit@gmail.com and let me know what you didn't like! Perhaps I can change it. In today's world, a book doesn't have to be stagnant, it can improve with time and feedback from readers like you. You can impact this book, and I welcome your feedback. Help make this book better for everyone!